AAT

TECHNICIAN

COMBINED COMPANION Unit 19

Preparing Personal Taxation Computations
(Finance Act 2005)

For exams in June 2006 and
December 2006

BPP PROFESSIONAL EDUCATION®

First edition February 2005
Second edition August 2005

ISBN 07517 2373 8 (Previous edition 0 7517 1644 8)

British Library Cataloguing-in-Publication Data
A catalogue record for this book is available from the British Library

Published by

BPP Professional Education
Aldine House,
Aldine Place,
London, W12 8AW

Printed in Great Britain by WM Print
Frederick Street
Walsall
West Midlands
WS2 9NE

CONTENTS

Course Companion

Revision Companion

Practice exams

INTRODUCTION

This is the second edition of BPP's Combined Companion for AAT Unit 19: Preparing Personal Taxation Computations. It has been carefully designed to enable students to practise all aspects of the requirements of the Standards of Competence and performance criteria, and ultimately be successful in their exam.

There is a Course Companion section containing these key features:

- clear, step by step explanation of the topic
- logical progression from one topic to the next
- numerous illustrations and practical examples
- interactive activities within the Course Companion itself, with answers supplied
- a bank of questions of varying complexity again with answers supplied.

The Revision Companion section contains:

- graded activities corresponding to each chapter of the Course Companion, with answers
- five practice exams with answers. The Sample Simulation, December 2003, June 2004 and December 2004 papers are included. BPP have written their own answers to these exams.

All material has been fully updated to reflect the Finance Acts 2005.

Tax forms

In your exam you may have take information from Forms P60 and P11D. We have included these forms within this Course Companion for illustrative purposes.

In addition you may have to complete the following supplementary pages to the tax return form:

- Employment income
- Property income.

You can practise using these forms when you try the practice exams in this Course Companion.

Please note that at the time this Course Companion was printed 2005/06 versions of these pages were not available. We have therefore updated the 2004/05 versions of the forms and amended them where necessary to fit in with Finance Act 2005/06 tax legislation. This necessarily involves us in making 'guesses' about how the 2005/06 forms will change. Although, it is unlikely that the 2005/06 versions of the forms will differ significantly from what we have included here, it is important that you contact the Revenue for updated copies before you sit your examination.

If you have internet access you should be able to find the 2005/06 forms on the Revenue's website (www.hmrc.gov.UK).

UNIT 19 STANDARDS OF COMPETENCE AND PERFORMANCE CRITERIA

The structure of the standards of Unit 19

The Unit commences with a statement of the knowledge and understanding which underpin competence in the Unit's elements.

The Unit of Competence is then divided into elements of competence describing activities which the individual should be able to perform.

Each element includes:

a) A set of performance criteria. This defines what constitutes competent performance.

b) A range statement. This defines the situations, contexts, methods etc in which competence should be displayed.

The elements of competence for Unit 19: Preparing Personal Taxation Computations are set out below. Knowledge and understanding required for the Unit as a whole are listed first, followed by the performance criteria and range statements for each element.

UNIT 19 PREPARING PERSONAL TAXATION COMPUTATIONS

What is the unit about?

This unit is about preparing tax computations and returns for individuals. It is concerned with the Income Tax and Capital Gains Tax liability of employed individuals, and also of self?employed individuals excluding any calculation of their business income. There are four elements in this unit.

The first element requires you to calculate income from employment, including the amount of taxable benefits.

In the second element you must calculate property and investment income and show that you can apply deductions and reliefs and claim loss set-offs.

The third element is concerned with preparing Income Tax computations, based on your calculations of the client's earned and unearned income.

The final element requires you to prepare Capital Gains Tax computations. As well as calculating chargeable gains and losses, you need to show that you apply reliefs and exemptions correctly.

Throughout the unit you must show that you take account of current tax law and Inland Revenue practice and make submissions within statutory timescales. You also need to show that you consult with the Revenue in an open and constructive manner, give timely and constructive advice to clients and maintain client confidentiality.

Knowledge and understanding

To perform this unit effectively you will need to know and understand:

The business environment

1 The duties and responsibilities of the tax practitioner (Elements 19.1, 19.2, 19.3 & 19.4)
2 The issues of taxation liability (Elements 19.1, 19.2, 19.3 & 19.4)
3 Relevant legislation and guidance from the Revenue (Elements 19.1, 19.2, 19.3 & 19.4)

Taxation principles and theory

4 Basic law and practice relating to all issues covered in the range and referred to in the performance criteria (Elements 19.1, 19.2, 19.3 & 19.4)

5 Calculation of assessable employment income including benefits (Element 19.1)

6 Expenses deductible from employment income including pension contributions and payroll giving to charities (Element 19.1)

7 Classification and calculation of income as property income, savings or dividend income (Element 19.2)

8 Identification of the main tax exempt investments (Element 19.2)

9 Calculation and set-off of rental deficits (Element 19.2)

10 Computation of taxable income taking account of gift aid payments and personal allowances for taxpayers aged under 65 (Element 19.3)

11 Calculation of tax on general, savings and dividend income (Element 19.3)

12 Identification of non-business assets disposed of including part disposals and personal shareholdings (Element 19.4)

13 Calculation of gains and losses on disposals of non-business assets including indexation allowance (Element 19.4)

14 Set-off of capital losses, taper relief and annual exemption to arrive at taxable gains (Element 19.4)

15 Calculation of capital gains tax payable on gains on non-business assets disposed of by individuals (Element 19.4)

16 Self assessment including payment of tax and filing of returns by individuals (Elements 19.3 & 19.4)

The client

17 How the taxation liabilities of individuals are affected by their employment status (Elements 19.1, 19.2, 19.3 & 19.4)

18 An understanding of the individual's employment status (Elements 19.1, 19.2, 19.3 & 19.4)

Element 19.1 Calculate income from employment

Performance criteria	**Chapter(s)**
In order to perform this element successfully you need to:	
■ Prepare accurate computations of emoluments, including benefits	3
■ List allowable expenses and deductions	3
■ Record relevant details of income from employment accurately and legibly in the tax return	4
■ Make computations and submissions in accordance with current tax law and take account of current Revenue practice	3, 4
■ Consult with Revenue staff in an open and constructive manner	3, 4
■ Give timely and constructive advice to clients on the recording of information relevant to tax returns	10
■ Maintain client confidentiality at all times	10

Range statement

Performance in this element relates to the following contexts:

- Emoluments
  - Received by UK-resident employees
  - Relating to work performed wholly or partly in the UK
- Benefits
  - Excluded employees
  - Other employees
- Allowable expenses
  - Contributions to pension schemes
  - Contributions to charities under the payroll deduction scheme

Element 19.2 Calculate property and investment income

Performance criteria	**Chapter(s)**
In order to perform this element successfully you need to:	
■ Prepare schedules of dividends and interest received on shares and securities	1
■ Prepare schedules of property income and determine profits and losses	5
■ Prepare schedules of investment income from other sources	1
■ Apply deductions and reliefs and claim loss set-offs	1, 5

	Chapter(s)
■ Record relevant details of property and investment income accurately and legibly in the tax return	5
■ Make computations and submissions in accordance with current tax law and take account of current Inland Revenue practice	1, 5
■ Consult with Revenue staff in an open and constructive manner	1, 5
■ Give timely and constructive advice to clients on the recording of information relevant to tax returns	10
■ Maintain client confidentiality at all times	10

Range statement

Performance in this element relates to the following contexts:

- Property income taking into account
  - Holiday lets
  - Wear and tear
- Other sources of investment income
  - Banks
  - Building societies
  - Government savings schemes

Element 19.3 Prepare Income Tax computations

Performance criteria	**Chapter(s)**
In order to perform this element successfully you need to:	
■ List general income, savings income and dividend income and check for completeness	1
■ Calculate and deduct charges and personal allowances	1
■ Calculate Income Tax payable	2
■ Record income and payments legibly and accurately in the tax return	4, 5, 10
■ Make computations and submissions in accordance with current tax law and take account of current Inland Revenue practice	1–5
■ Consult with Revenue staff in an open and constructive manner	1–5
■ Give timely and constructive advice to clients on the recording of information relevant to tax returns	10
■ Maintain client confidentiality at all times	10

Range statement

Performance in this element relates to the following contexts:

There are no additional contextual requirements in this element.

Element 19.4 Prepare Capital Gains Tax computations

Performance criteria	**Chapter(s)**
In order to perform this element successfully you need to:	
■ Identify and value disposed-of chargeable personal assets	6–9
■ Identify shares disposed of by individuals	8
■ Calculate chargeable gains and allowable losses	6–9
■ Apply reliefs and exemptions correctly	6–9
■ Calculate Capital Gains Tax payable	6
■ Record relevant details of gains and the Capital Gains Tax payable legibly and accurately in the tax return	10
■ Make computations and submissions in accordance with current tax law and take account of current Inland Revenue practice	6–10
■ Consult with Revenue staff in an open and constructive manner	10
■ Give timely and constructive advice to clients on the recording of information relevant to tax returns	10
■ Maintain client confidentiality at all times	10

Range statement

Performance in this element relates to the following contexts:

- Chargeable personal assets that have been
  - Sold
  - Gifted
  - Lost
  - Destroyed

ASSESSMENT STRATEGY

This Unit is assessed by exam based assessment only.

Exam based assessment

An exam based assessment is a means of collecting evidence that you have the essential knowledge and understanding which underpins competence. It is also a means of collecting evidence across the range of contexts for the standards, and of your ability to transfer skills, knowledge and understanding to different situations. Thus, although exams contain practical tests linked to the performance criteria, they also focus on the underpinning knowledge and understanding. You should, in addition, expect each exam to contain tasks taken from across a broad range of the standards.

Format of exam

There will be a three hour exam in two sections.

Section 1: Element 19.1 (taxation of an individual who is employed)
Section 2: Element 19.4 (taxation of capital transactions)

Elements 19.2 and 19.3 can appear in either section.

There will be an additional 15 minutes reading time.

TAX RATES AND ALLOWANCES

A Income tax

1 Rates

	2004/05		2005/06	
	£	%	£	%
Starting rate	1 – 2,020	10	1 – 2,090	10
Basic rate	2,021 – 31,400	22	2,091 – 32,400	22
Higher rate	31,401 and above	40	32,401 and above	40

Savings (excluding dividend) income is taxed at 20% if it falls in the basic rate band. Dividend income in both the starting rate and the basic rate bands is taxed at 10%. Dividend income within the higher rate band is taxed at 32.5%.

2 Allowances

	2004/05	2005/06
	£	£
Personal allowance	4,745	4,895

3 Car Benefit

Baseline CO_2 Emissions = 140g/km

4 Car fuel charge – 2005/06

Set figure £14,400

5 Authorised mileage rates (AMR) 2005/06 rates

Car mileage rates

First 10,000 miles	40p per mile
Over 10,000 miles	25p per mile

Bicycles	*Motor cycles*
20p per mile	24p per mile
Passenger payments	5p per mile

B Capital gains tax

1 Annual exemption (individuals)

	£
2004/05	8,200
2005/06	8,500

2 Tapering relief for non-business assets

Number of complete years after 5 April 1998 for which asset held	*Business assets % of gain chargeable*
0	100
1	100
2	100
3	95
4	90
5	85
6	80
7	75
8	70
9	65
10 or more	60

COURSE COMPANION UNIT 19

chapter 1: INTRODUCTION

chapter coverage

In this chapter we see that individuals pay income tax on their income and capital gains tax on their chargeable gains. We then see that the rules governing these taxes are laid down in both Acts of Parliament and a body of law known as case law.

Finally we see how to compute an individual's taxable income. This is the most important part of this chapter as you will almost certainly have to compute taxable income in your exam.

The topics that we shall cover are:

- Taxes paid by individuals
- Relevant legislation and guidance from the Revenue
- Computation of taxable income

KNOWLEDGE AND UNDERSTANDING AND PERFORMANCE CRITERIA COVERAGE

knowledge and understanding

- The issues of taxation liability (Elements 19.1, 19.2, 19.3, 19.4)
- Relevant legislation and guidance from the Revenue (Elements 19.1, 19.2, 19.3, 19.4)
- Basic law and practice (Elements 19.1, 19.2, 19.3, 19.4)
- Classification and calculation of income as property income, savings or dividend income (Element 19.2)
- Identification of the main tax exempt investments (Element 19.2)
- Computation of taxable income taking account of gift aid payments and personal allowances for taxpayers aged under 65 (Element 19.3)

Performance criteria

- Prepare schedules of dividend and interest received on shares and securities
- Prepare schedules of investment income from other sources
- List general income, savings income and dividend income and check for completeness
- Calculate and deduct charges and personal allowances

student notes

TAXES PAID BY INDIVIDUALS

Individuals must pay income tax on their taxable income and capital gains tax on any taxable gains arising on the disposal of chargeable assets. You will study income tax in the first part of this Course Companion and capital gains tax in the second part of this Course Companion.

As a general rule, income is a receipt that is expected to recur (such as employment income), whereas a gain is a one off profit on the disposal of a capital asset (e.g. the profit on the sale of a property held as an investment).

RELEVANT LEGISLATION AND GUIDANCE FROM THE REVENUE

Most of the rules governing the above taxes are laid down in various Acts of parliament. These Acts are collectively known as the Tax Legislation. The existing Acts are normally amended each year in the annual Finance Act. However, in 2005 we have two Finance Acts because of the dissolution of Parliament in April 2005, in preparation for the General Election in May 2005. This Course Companion includes the provisions of both the Finance Act 2005 and the Finance (No 2) Act 2005. These Acts will be examined in June 2006 and December 2006.

To help taxpayers, the Revenue publish a wide range of guidance material on how they interpret the various Acts. Much of this information can be found on the Revenue's website, www.hmrc.gov.uk. However, none of the Revenue's guidance material has the force of law. Although, you may like to have a look at this website, you should find all you need for exam purposes within this Course Companion.

Sometimes there may be a disagreement between the Revenue and a taxpayer as to how a certain part of the tax legislation should be interpreted. In this case either the taxpayer or the Revenue may take the case to court.

Cases decided by the court provide guidance on how legislation should be interpreted and collectively form a second source of tax law known as case law. You will not be expected to quote the names of decided cases in your exam but you may need to know the principle decided in a case. Where relevant this will be mentioned within this Course Companion.

COMPUTATION OF TAXABLE INCOME

An individual may receive various different types of income such as income from employment, rental income, interest, dividends and/or income from a business. All of this income must be brought together in a personal tax computation.

student notes

Individuals must prepare personal tax computations for tax years. A TAX YEAR, FISCAL YEAR or YEAR OF ASSESSMENT is the year that runs from 6 April in one year to 5 April in the next. For example, the 2005/06 tax year runs from 6 April 2005 to 5 April 2006. The 2006 exams will be based on the tax law that applies for the 2005/06 tax year.

An individual's income from all sources must be brought together in the personal tax computation. In this computation income must be split into three types:

a) NON-SAVINGS INCOME
b) SAVINGS (EXCLUDING DIVIDEND) INCOME, and
c) DIVIDEND INCOME

Non-savings income is all income other than interest and dividends. Savings (excluding dividend) income is interest. Dividend income includes all dividends from UK companies.

The total of an individual's income from all sources less charges on income (see below) is known as STATUTORY TOTAL INCOME.

All persons (including children) are entitled to the personal allowance (PA) of £4,895 in 2005/06. The personal allowance is deducted from STI to arrive at taxable income. The allowance comes off non-savings income first, then off savings (excluding dividend) income and lastly off dividend income.

The example below shows the layout of the taxable income computation:

Taxable income for 2005/06

	Non-savings income	*Savings (excluding dividend) income*	*Dividend income*	*Total*
	£	£	£	£
Employment income	30,000			
Interest		1,000		
UK dividends			1,000	
Statutory total income (STI)	30,000	1,000	1,000	32,000
Less: personal allowance	(4,895)			
Taxable income	25,105	1,000	1,000	27,105

Now follow the above layout to try the next activity for yourself.

student notes

Activity 1

An individual has the following types of income in 2005/06.

	£
Business income	44,000
Building society interest (gross – see below)	2,000
Dividends (gross – see below)	1,000

Show his taxable income split into non-savings, savings (excluding dividend) and dividend income.

Interest income

Individuals usually receive bank and building society interest net of 20% tax. This means that the bank/building society deducts 20% tax from the payment made to the individual and pays that tax to the Revenue on the individual's behalf.

Interest must be included gross in the income tax computation. This means that if interest is received net, it must be grossed up for inclusion in the income tax computation. For example, interest received of £80 must be grossed up to £100 (£80 × 100/80). The tax suffered on the interest income of £20 can be offset against the individual's income tax payable. If it exceeds the tax payable the excess can be repaid. We will see how to compute income tax payable in the next chapter.

In the exam you may be given either the net or the gross amount of interest: read the question carefully. If you are given the net amount (the amount received or credited), you should gross up the figure as shown above. However, if you are given the gross amount include the figure you are given in the income tax computation.

Activity 2

In 2005/06 Jesse receives bank account interest of £160. What amount of interest must be included in Jesse's income tax computation?

Dividends

Dividends are always received net of a 10% tax credit. This means a dividend received of £90 has a £10 tax credit, giving gross income of £100 to be included in the tax computation. The tax credit attached to dividends cannot be repaid to non-taxpayers but it can be offset against a taxpayer's tax liability. We will see how to compute a taxpayer's tax liability in the next chapter.

student notes

Activity 3

Maria receives dividends of £900 and building society interest of £1,600 in 2005/06. What are the gross amounts of dividends and interest to be included in her income tax computation for 2005/06?

Exempt income

Some income is exempt from income tax. You should not include this income in the income tax computation. The only type of exempt income that you will meet in your exam is income arising on Individual Savings accounts (ISAs)

In your exam you should always state that this income is exempt. If you do not you may not be awarded the available mark.

Charges on income

A CHARGE ON INCOME is a payment which income tax law allows as a deduction.

The two charges on income that you may meet in Unit 19 are:

a) patent royalties
b) copyright royalties

These royalties are deducted in computing statutory total income. They are deducted firstly from non-savings income, then from savings (excluding dividend) income and finally from dividend income.

Copyright royalties are paid gross. However, patent royalties are paid net of 22% tax. This means that the payer withholds 22% tax from the payment of a patent royalty and pays it over to the Revenue on the recipient's behalf.

You must always deduct the gross figure in the personal tax computation. Gross a patent royalty paid up by multiplying by 100/78. For example if Kahlida pays a patent royalty of £780 you must gross it up to £1,000 (£780 × 100/78) and deduct the gross figure in Kahlida's income tax computation.

Activity 4

In 2005/06 Zak pays a patent royalty of £390 and a copyright royalty of £200. What is the total amount that Zak can deduct as charges on income in his income tax computation for 2005/06?

If you are preparing the personal tax computation of someone who receives a royalty, for example the owner of a patent who gets royalties from someone who exploits the patent, include the gross amount under non-savings income. If the royalty is a copyright royalty, the gross amount is the amount received. If the royalty is a patent royalty the gross amount is the amount received × 100/78.

CHAPTER OVERVIEW

- Individuals may have to pay income tax and/or capital gains tax. Some of the rules governing these taxes are laid down in Tax Legislation whilst some are laid down in case law
- Tax computations must be prepared for a tax year
- All of an individual's income is added together, and charges on income are deducted, to arrive at statutory total income
- A personal allowance is deducted from statutory total income to arrive at taxable income. For 2005/06 all individuals are entitled to a personal allowance of £4,895
- Personal allowances and charges on income are deducted firstly from non-savings income, then from savings (excluding dividend) income and finally from dividend income
- Individuals receive most interest net of 20% tax. Gross interest up by multiplying by 100/80
- Dividends are received net of a 10% tax credit. Gross dividends up by multiplying by 100/90
- Patent royalties paid/received must be grossed up by multiplying by 100/78
- Always include gross figures in the income tax computation
- Income arising on an Individual Savings Account is exempt from income tax. It must not be included in the income tax computation.

KEY WORDS

The **Tax Year**, **Year of Assessment** or **Fiscal Year** is the year that runs from 6 April in one year to 5 April in the next year.

Non-savings income is all income other than interest and dividends

Savings (excluding dividend) income is all interest

Dividend income is all dividend income received from UK companies

Statutory total income is the total of an individual's income from all sources less charges on income

Taxable income is an individual's statutory total income minus the personal allowance

A **charge on income** is a payment by the taxpayer which income tax law allows as a deduction

HOW MUCH HAVE YOU LEARNED?

1 What amounts must be included in the personal tax computation in respect of the following:

a) building society interest received of £240
b) interest received on an individual savings account of £40
c) dividends received of £144

2 Joe has employment income of £30,000 and receives dividends of £270 in 2005/06. What is his taxable income for 2005/06?

3 Pratish receives rental income of £3,000 and building society interest of £7,200 in 2005/06. What is his taxable income for 2005/06?

4 Jesse has business profits of £20,000 in 2005/06. He also received building society interest of £4,000 and dividends of £3,600. He paid a patent royalty of £3,020. What is Jesse's taxable income for 2005/06?

chapter 2: COMPUTING INCOME TAX PAYABLE

chapter coverage

In the last chapter you saw how to compute an individual's taxable income. In this chapter you will see how to compute the income tax payable on this income.

The topics that we shall cover are:

- Calculating the income tax liability
- Calculating income tax payable

KNOWLEDGE AND UNDERSTANDING AND PERFORMANCE CRITERIA COVERAGE

knowledge and understanding

- The issues of taxation liability (Elements 19.1, 19.2, 19.3, 19.4)
- Calculation of tax on general, savings and dividend income (Element 19.3)

Performance criteria

- Calculate Income Tax payable

student notes

CALCULATING THE INCOME TAX LIABILITY

Income tax bands

In the last chapter we saw how to compute taxable income. The first step in calculating the income tax liability on this taxable income is to divide the total taxable income into three bands:

a) the first £2,090 of income; this is called income in the STARTING RATE BAND

b) the next £30,310 of income; this is income in the BASIC RATE BAND

c) the remaining income over the HIGHER RATE THRESHOLD of £32,400

The bands and the higher rate threshold given above are the bands/threshold that apply in 2005/06. The figures will be different in different tax years. You will be given the figures necessary for your exam in the tax rates and allowances on the exam paper.

The rate of tax applied to the income in each band depends on whether the income is non-savings income, interest income or dividend income.

There is only one set of income tax bands used for all three types of income. These bands must be allocated to income in the following order:

a) non-savings income
b) savings (excluding dividend) income
c) dividend income

We will look at this below.

Computing the tax liability

You need to calculate the tax due on taxable income in four steps:

Step 1: Deal with non-savings income first:

Non-savings income in the starting rate band is taxed at 10%. Next any non-savings income in the basic rate band is taxed at 22%. Finally non-savings income above the higher rate threshold is taxed at 40%.

Step 2: Secondly, deal with savings (excluding dividend) income:

Savings (excluding dividend) income is dealt with after non-savings income. If any of the starting or basic rate bands remain after taxing non-savings income they can be used here.

student notes

Savings (excluding dividend) income is taxed at 10% in the starting rate band. Savings (excluding dividend) income that falls within the basic rate band is taxed at 20% (not 22%). Once interest income is above the higher rate threshold, it is taxed at 40%.

Step 3: Thirdly, compute tax on dividend income:

Lastly, tax dividend income. If dividend income falls within the starting or basic rate bands, it is taxed at 10% (never 20% or 22%). If, however, the dividend income exceeds the higher rate threshold of £31,400, it is taxed at 32.5%

Step 4: Add income tax retained on patent royalties paid net

The final step in computing the tax liability should be to add on any tax withheld from patent royalties paid in the year. You should recall from the previous chapter that patent royalties are paid net of 22% tax. This tax withheld must be added back on to the individual's tax liability.

How it works

Sasha has total taxable income of £40,000. Of this £30,400 is non-savings income, £2,600 is interest and £7,000 is dividend income.

The first £2,090 of non-savings income is in the starting rate band. The remaining £28,310 (£30,400 – £2,090) of non-savings income is in the basic rate band. £2,000 of the interest uses the remaining basic rate band. £600 of interest and all the dividends are above the higher rate threshold of £32,400.

The tax liability is:

		Income tax
		£
Step 1:	**Non savings income**	
	£2,090 × 10%	209
	£28,310 × 22%	6,228
Step 2:	**Savings (excluding dividend) income**	
	£2,000 × 20%	400
	£600 × 40%	240
Step 3:	**Dividend income**	
	£7,000 × 32.5%	2,275
Tax liability		9,352

Note. There are no patent royalties paid in the year so there is no step 4 in this case.

student notes

Activity 1

Talet has total taxable income of £60,000 for 2005/06. £25,000 of her taxable income is non-savings income. The remaining £35,000 is savings (excluding dividend) income. What is the total income tax liability?

Extending the basic rate band

We have seen above that an individual normally has a basic rate band of £30,310 in 2005/06. There are two circumstances in which the basic rate band must be increased. These are when the individual pays:

a) a gift aid donation, or
b) a premium to a personal pension scheme

A gift aid donation is a particular type of donation to charity on which tax relief is available.

Both gift aid donations and premiums to personal pension schemes are paid net of 22% tax. For example, this means that if an individual pays a gift aid donation of £780, the gross amount of the donation is £780 × 100/78 = £1,000.

The basic rate band is increased by the gross amount of a gift aid donation and/or the gross amount of any personal pension premium paid.

How it works

Gustav has taxable income (all non savings) of £43,000 on 2005/06. He received no other income in the year but he did pay a gift aid donation of £7,800.

Compute Gustav's income tax liability.

Solution

The gift aid donation will have been paid net of 22% tax. This means that the gross amount of the payment is £7,800 × 100/78 = £10,000 and Gustav's basic rate band must be extended by £10,000. His income tax liability is calculated as follows:

	£
£2,090 × 10%	209
£30,310 × 22%	6,668
£10,000 (Extended band) × 22%	2,200
£600 × 40%	240
	9,317

student notes

Activity 2

In 2005/06 Hans has taxable income of £40,000. £22,000 of taxable income is non-savings income, the rest is savings (excluding dividend) income. Hans pays a personal pension premium of £5,460 in the 2005/06. Calculate Hans' tax liability for 2005/06.

An individual obtains basic rate tax relief on gift aid donations and personal pension premiums by paying them net. Extending the basic rate band gives additional tax relief.

CALCULATING INCOME TAX PAYABLE

We have seen above how to calculate the income tax liability on non-savings, savings (excluding dividend) and dividend income. Once this is done there are two final steps to be made in order to compute the tax payable:

Step 5: Deduct the tax credit on dividends from the tax liability. Although deductible, this tax credit cannot be repaid if it exceeds the tax liability calculated so far.

Step 6: Finally deduct any tax deducted at source from savings (excluding dividend) income and any PAYE (PAYE is the tax deducted at source from an individual's earnings: it will be covered later in this Course Companion).

These amounts of tax suffered can be repaid to the extent that they exceed the income tax liability.

The resulting figure is the tax payable which is the balance of the liability still to be settled in cash.

How it works

Samantha, has the following income and outgoings for 2005/06.

	£
Salary (tax deducted under PAYE £4,000)	25,000
UK dividend received (net)	2,000
Building society interest received (net)	12,400
Qualifying charitable donations paid under gift-aid (gross amount)	800

What is Samantha's tax due for 2005/06?

student notes

Solution

	Non-savings income	Savings (excluding dividend) income	Dividends	Total
	£	£	£	£
Employment income	25,000			
Building Society interest (BSI) £12,400 × 100/80		15,500		
UK dividends £2,000 × 100/90			2,222	
STI	25,000	15,500	2,222	42,722
Less: PA	(4,895)			
Taxable income	20,105	15,500	2,222	37,827

		£
Tax on non-savings income		
£2,090 × 10%		209
£18,015 × 22%		3,963
Tax on savings (excluding dividend) income		
£12,295 £(32,400 – 20,105) × 20%		2,459
£800 × 20%		160
£2,405 × 40%		962
Tax on dividend income		
£2,222 × 32.5%		722
		8,475
Less: tax credit on dividend income (£2,222 × 10%)		(222)
Less: income tax suffered		
PAYE	4,000	
tax on interest (£15,500 × 20%)	3,100	
		(7,100)
Income tax payable		1,153

Tutorial note. The basic rate band is extended by the gross amount of the gift aid donation.

Activity 3

In 2005/06 Barry has rental income of £20,000, bank interest (net amount received) of £8,000, and UK dividends received of £10,800. Compute Barry's income tax payable for 2005/06.

CHAPTER OVERVIEW

- We categorise income into different types; non-savings; savings (excluding dividend) and dividends. Each type of income suffers different rates of tax depending on whether the income falls into the starting, basic or higher rate band.
- There is one set of income tax bands that applies to all the income.
- Non-savings income is taxed first (at 10% then 22% then 40%) then savings (excluding dividend) income (at 10%, 20% then 40%) and finally dividend income (at 10%, 10% and 32.5%).

KEY WORDS

The first £2,090 of taxable income is income in the **starting rate band**

The next £30,310 of income is income in the **basic rate band**. The basic rate band may be extended by the gross amount of any gift aid donations and personal pension premiums paid.

The **higher rate threshold** is the threshold over which income is taxed at the higher rates.

- Gift aid donations and personal pension premiums are paid net of basic rate (22%) tax.
- Extend the basic rate band by the gross amount of any gift aid donations or personal pension premiums paid. This gives additional tax relief to higher rate taxpayers.
- Deduct the tax credit on dividend income from income tax payable. However, if it exceeds the income tax payable, the excess cannot be repaid.
- Tax suffered on interest and PAYE tax is deducted in computing tax payable and can be repaid.

HOW MUCH HAVE YOU LEARNED?

1 At what rates is income tax charged on non-savings income?

2 In 2005/06 Carol has a salary of £4,000, building society interest of £12,800 and a UK dividend of £18,000. Compute Carol's income tax liability.

3 In 2005/06, Albert has a salary of £10,000, £2,000 (gross) of building society interest and £3,000 (gross) of UK dividends. Compute Albert's income tax liability.

4 How is tax relief given on gift aid donations?

5 Doreen has the following sources of income in 2005/06.

	£
Income from employment (PAYE suffered £2,594)	17,000
Income from rented properties	3,500
Interest received on bank account (gross)	3,800
UK dividends received	6,500

Calculate Doreen's income tax payable for the year.

6 Sase has the following income and outgoings in 2005/06.

	£
Business profits	29,000
Building society interest received	4,000
UK dividends received	6,500
Gift aid donation paid	1,560

Compute Sase's income tax payable for the year.

chapter 3: EMPLOYMENT INCOME

chapter coverage

In this chapter you will start your studies of the calculation of employment income. We begin by considering how to decide whether an individual is employed or self-employed. We then learn how to calculate taxable earnings.

Finally we see how to calculate the taxable value of employer provided benefits.

We continue studying the calculation of employment income in the next chapter.

The topics that we shall cover are:

- Employment and self-employment
- Calculations of employment income
- Benefits: General charging provisions
- Benefits taxable on all employees
- Benefits taxable only on 'other' employees
- Exempt benefits

KNOWLEDGE AND UNDERSTANDING AND PERFORMANCE CRITERIA COVERAGE

knowledge and understanding

- The issues of taxation liability (Elements 19.1, 19.2, 19.3, 19.4)
- Basic law and practice (Elements 19.1, 19.2, 19.3, 19.4)
- Calculation of assessable employment income including benefits (Element 19.1)
- Expenses deductible from employment income including pension contributions and payroll giving to charity (Element 19.1)
- How the tax liabilities of individuals are affected by their employment status (Elements 19.1, 19.2, 19.3, 19.4)
- An understanding of an individual's employment status (Elements 19.1, 19.2, 19.3, 19.4)

Performance criteria

- Prepare accurate computations of emoluments, including benefits
- List allowable expenses and deductions

EMPLOYMENT AND SELF-EMPLOYMENT

student notes

It is important to be able to distinguish between employment (Employment Income) and self employment (Business profits). However, the distinction is a fine one. Employment is a contract of service, whereas self-employment is a contract for services.

It used to be thought that the deciding factor was the degree of control exercised by one party over the other. The most that can be said now, however, is that control will always have to be considered, although it can no longer be regarded as the sole determining factor; other factors which may be of importance are such matters as:

a) whether the person performing the services provides his own equipment;

b) whether he hires his own helpers;

c) what degree of financial risk he takes;

d) what degree of responsibility for investment and management he has; and

e) whether and how far he has an opportunity of profiting from sound management in the performance of his task.

In other words, the fundamental test to be applied is whether the person performing the services is performing them as a person in business on his own account. You may need to look at all of the above factors and form a view based on the balance of the evidence.

TAXATION OF EMPLOYMENT INCOME

Earnings from an office or employment are taxed as employment income.

Earnings include:

a) salaries, bonuses and commissions
b) any benefits provided by the employer, and
c) payments made on the termination of employment

We will look at these three types of earnings in this and the next chapter.

Certain allowable deductions can be deducted in the calculation of taxable earnings.

student notes✍

ALLOWABLE DEDUCTIONS

The following expenditure can be deducted in the calculation of taxable earnings:

a) contributions to an approved occupational pension scheme (we look at pension contributions in detail in the next chapter);

b) subscriptions to professional bodies, if relevant to the duties of employment;

c) donations to charity under an approved payroll deduction scheme. A payroll giving scheme is a charitable giving scheme operated by an employer;

d) qualifying travel expenses; and

(e) other expenses incurred wholly, exclusively and necessarily in the performance of the duties of employment.

Qualifying travel expenses

Travel expenses are deductible if they are either incurred

a) on business travel, or

b) on travelling to a temporary workplace. A workplace is temporary if the employee will return to his normal workplace at the end of a temporary period and the temporary period lasts for less than 24 months.

Travel to work is not allowable.

If an employee uses his own vehicle for business travel, the cost (to the extent that it is not reimbursed) can be claimed as a deduction. The cost of private mileage (eg from home to a permanent workplace) is not deductible. Any claim must be based on the mileage rates in the tax legislation. These rates are the Revenue's authorised mileage rates. If necessary, these rates will be given to you on the exam paper.

How it works

Patrick uses his own car for work. During 2005/06 he travelled 14,000 miles on his employer's business. Patrick's employer did not reimburse any amounts spent in respect of the business mileage. What amount can be deducted in calculating taxable earnings?

The statutory mileage rates are 40p for the first 10,000 miles and 25p, thereafter.

student notes

Solution

	£
10,000 × 40p	4,000
4,000 × 25p	1,000
Deductible amount	5,000

We look, below, at the consequences that arise if the employer pays an employee an allowance to cover the cost of business mileage.

Expenses incurred wholly, exclusively and necessarily in the performance of the duties of an employment

This test of deductiblilty is applied quite strictly. For example, none of the cost of renting a phone line is deductible if the phone is also used for private purposes. This is because the line is not used 'exclusively' for business purposes. Strictly, any other expenses that have a private element are not deductible but, in practice, taxpayers are usually allowed to apportion expenses between parts that are for private purposes and those that are for business purposes. The business part of an expense is deductible.

BENEFITS: GENERAL CHARGING PROVISIONS

To calculate the value of employer provided benefits, employees must be divided into two groups:

a) EXCLUDED EMPLOYEES; and
b) 'other' employees.

Excluded employees are employees, who are not directors, and who earn at the rate of less than £8,500 per annum.

In general:

a) a benefit received by an excluded employee is taxable only if it can be turned into money. The value of such a benefit is the amount that it would fetch if the employee were to dispose of it to a third party (often known as the benefit's 'SECOND-HAND VALUE').

b) the value of a benefit provided to 'other' employees is the cost to the employer of providing that benefit.

For both types of employee there are many specific rules, which override the above rules. We look at these below.

student notes

BENEFITS TAXABLE ON ALL EMPLOYEES

Vouchers

An employee who receives:

a) non-cash vouchers (eg book tokens); or
b) credit tokens (eg a credit card)

is normally taxable on the cost to the employer of providing the benefit.

If an employee receives a cash voucher, he will be taxable on the amount for which the voucher can be exchanged.

Accommodation

If an employer provides an employee with accommodation, there is a basic benefit equal to the higher of:

a) the 'annual value' of the property (given in the exam); and

b) any rent actually paid for the property by the employer (if the property is rented rather than owned by the employer).

The benefit is reduced by any contribution the employee makes for the use of the property.

How it works

Tony is provided with a company flat

	£
Annual value	300
Rent paid by the company	3,380
Amount paid by Tony to the company for the use of the flat	520

Calculate Tony's taxable benefit.

Solution

		£
Benefit: greater of:		
a) annual value	£300	
b) rent paid	£3,380	
ie		3,380
Less: reimbursed to the company		(520)
Net benefit		2,860

student notes

If the cost of employer-provided accommodation exceeds £75,000, an additional benefit arises. The amount of the additional benefit is equal to:

ORI × (C – £75,000)

ORI is the official rate of interest at the start of the tax year. This will be given to you in the exam.

C is the cost of providing the accommodation. This includes the cost of purchase and the cost of any improvements made before the start of the tax year.

If the accommodation was acquired by the employer more than six years before it was first provided to the employee and its original cost plus improvements exceeded £75,000, the 'cost of providing' is increased (or reduced if appropriate) to its market value when first provided to that employee.

Where any contribution paid by the employee exceeds the annual value of the property, the excess may be deducted from the further benefit.

How it works

Simon's employer provided him with a house throughout 2005/06. The company bought the house for £133,000 on 1 April 2001.

For 2005/06, the annual value of the house is £1,400. Simon pays £3,000 for the use of the house to his employer.

Calculate the total benefit for 2005/06 arising in respect of the house. Assume the official rate of interest is 5%.

Solution

Basic charge:

	£
Annual value	1,400
Less: contribution	(1,400)
	NIL

Additional charge:

	£	£
Cost	133,000	
Less:	(75,000)	
Excess	58,000	
£58,000 × 5%		2,900
Less: contribution (£3,000 – 1,400)		(1,600)
Total benefit 2005/06		1,300

student notes

Activity 1

Throughout 2005/06 Marak lived in a house provided by his employer. The following information is relevant:

Annual value	£5,200
Cost of the house (bought by employer in 2004)	£600,000
Rent paid by Marak in 2005/06	£12,000
Official rate of interest throughout 2005/06	5%

Calculate the taxable value of the accommodation provided in 2005/06.

Mileage allowances

Where employers pay mileage allowances to employees who use their own vehicles for business travel, the employees are taxed on any amounts received in excess of the statutory mileage rates. The statutory mileage rates for cars are 40p a mile for the first 10,000 miles and 25p a mile thereafter. There are separate mileage rates for motorcycles and bicycles. If you need any of these rates, they will be given to you in the exam.

As we saw above, if the allowance received by the employee is less than the cost calculated using the statutory rates the employee may deduct the shortfall when calculating taxable earnings.

How it works

Owen drives 14,000 business miles in 2005/06 using his own car.

You are required to calculate the taxable benefit/allowable deduction assuming:

a) He is reimbursed 40p a mile
b) He is reimbursed 25p a mile

Solution

		£
Statutory limit:	10,000 × 40p	4,000
	4,000 × 25p	1,000
		5,000

a)

	£
Amount received (14,000 × 40p)	5,600
Less: statutory limit	(5,000)
Taxable benefit	600

student notes

b)

	£
Amount received (14,000 × 25p)	3,500
Less: statutory limit	(5,000)
Allowable deduction	(1,500)

Activity 2

Yarrik used his car to travel 12,000 business miles in 2005/06. His employer paid him 38p per business mile travelled. What, if any, is the taxable benefit arising on Yarrik in respect of the amount paid to him by his employer?

BENEFITS TAXABLE ONLY ON 'OTHER' EMPLOYEES

The benefits below are taxable only on directors and employees earning at the rate of £8,500 per annum or more.

Company cars

If a car is provided for private use by reason of a person's employment a taxable benefit arises. The benefit is normally a percentage of the car's list price. The percentage for a car that emits up to 140 grams of carbon dioxide per kilometre is 15%. This percentage increases by one percentage point for every additional 5 grams/kilometre (g/km) of CO_2 emissions emitted, up to a maximum of 35%. The percentage is further increased by 3% for diesel cars (again up to the maximum of 35%).

You will always be given a car's CO_2 emission rate in your exam. Your first step in calculating a car benefit should be to round this down to the nearest 5g/km below the actual emissions. You then need to see by how many g/km the base figure of 140g/km is exceeded. We show how this works in the following example.

How it works

Nigel is provided with a petrol engined car which had a list price of £22,000. The car has CO_2 emissions of 203g/km.

Calculate Nigel's taxable car benefit for 2005/06.

student notes

Solution

Round down 203 g/km to 200 g/km

The amount by which the base figure is exceeded is 60g/km (200 – 140)

Increase the taxable percentage is by 1% for every 5g/km above the base figure, ie increase it by 60/5 = 12%.

Taxable percentage = 15% + 12% = 27%

Car benefit £22,000 ×27% = £5,940

If an employee makes a capital contribution towards the cost of a car, the contribution is deducted from the list price used for calculating the benefit, subject to a maximum deduction of £5,000. If, however, an employee makes a payment for the private use of a car (as distinct from a capital contribution to the cost of the car), the payment is deducted in calculating the taxable benefit.

The car benefit is pro-rated if the car is only provided for part of the year or if it is incapable of being used for 30 or more consecutive days.

How it works

Vicky starts her employment on 6 January 2006 and is immediately provided with a new petrol engined car with a list price of £25,000. The car was more expensive than her employer would have provided and she therefore made a capital contribution of £6,200. Vicky contributed £100 a month for being able to use the car privately. CO_2 emissions are 267g/km. Calculate the car benefit for 2005/06.

Solution

	£
List price	25,000
Less: capital contributions (maximum)	(5,000)
	20,000

£20,000 × 35% (W) = £7,000

	£
3/12 × £7,000	1,750
Less: contribution to running costs (£100 × 3)	(300)
Car benefit	1,450

Working

CO_2 emissions = 265 g/km (rounded down)

The amount by which the base figure is exceeded is 125 g/km (265 – 140)

125/5 = 25

Taxable percentage = 15% + 25% = 40% but restrict to 35% maximum.

The maximum list price or market value that can be used in calculating a taxable benefit is £80,000.

The taxable car benefit covers all expenditure by the employer on repairs, servicing, insurance, road fund licence and cleaning of the car. No additional benefit arises in respect of these items. A taxable benefit does, however, arise in respect of a chauffeur provided for private mileage. This will be based on the cost of the chauffeur.

student notes

Fuel provided for private use

If an employer pays for fuel used for private motoring in a company car, a fuel benefit arises.

The benefit is a percentage of a base figure. The base figure for 2005/06 is £14,400. The percentage is the same percentage as is used to calculate the car benefit.

No benefit arises where it can be shown that either all the fuel provided was used only for business travel or that the employee has reimbursed the whole of the expense of any fuel provided for his private use.

The fuel benefit is reduced if private fuel is not available for part of a tax year. However, if private fuel later becomes available in the same tax year, there is no reduction made.

How it works

An employee was provided with a new petrol engined car costing £15,000 (the list price) on 1 June 2005. During 2005/06 the employer spent £900 on insurance, repairs and the vehicle licence. The firm paid for all petrol (£2,300) without reimbursement. The employee was required to pay the firm £25 per month for the private use of the car.

The car has CO_2 emissions of 140g/km.

Calculate the total taxable benefit for 2005/06 in respect of the car and fuel.

student notes

Solution

Car was available for 10 months.

	£
List price £15,000 × 15%	2,250
£2,250 × 10/12	1,875
Less: contribution (10 × £25)	(250)
	1,625
Fuel benefit £14,400 × 15% × 10/12	1,800
Taxable benefit	3,425

If the contribution of £25 per month had been towards the petrol, the benefit assessable would have been £(1,875 + 1,800) = £3,675. Conversely, if the cost of private petrol were fully reimbursed by the employee then there would have been no fuel benefit at all.

Activity 3

Nissar had the use of a company car throughout 2005/06. The list price of the car was £30,000. The car was diesel engined and had CO_2 emissions of 199g/km. The company provided fuel for both private and business motoring. Nissar made a contribution of £400 towards the cost of private fuel.

What is the total taxable benefit arising to Nissar in 2005/06?

Private use of employer assets

If an employee uses an employer asset (other than a car or accommodation) an annual benefit arises equal to 20% of the market value of the asset when first used by the employee.

If the asset is subsequently acquired by the employee, the benefit arising on the acquisition is usually the greater of:

a) the market value of the asset on acquisition; and

b) the market value of the asset when first provided to the employee less any amounts already assessed as a benefit.

How it works

A suit costing £200 is bought by an employer for use by an employee on 6 April 2004. On 6 April 2005 the suit is purchased by the employee for £15, its market value then being £25.

What is the taxable benefit in 2005/06?

student notes

Solution

The benefit taxable in 2004/05 will be 20% × £200 = £40

The benefit taxable in 2005/06 will be the greater of:

a) Market value at acquisition by employee = £25

b)

	£	£
Original market value	200	
Less: assessed in respect of use 2004/05	(40)	
	160	
ie		160
Less: price paid by employee		(15)
Taxable benefit 2005/06		145

Activity 4

Ahmed bought video equipment from his employer on 1 July 2005 for £1,000. The equipment was then worth £4,000. Ahmed had first used the equipment on 6 April 2004 when his employer had lent it to him for private use. The market value of the equipment was £6,000 on 6 April 2004.

Calculate any taxable benefits arising in 2004/05 and 2005/06.

Computers and Bicycles

There is an exception to the above rule for computers and bicycles which have previously been provided as exempt or partly exempt benefits. The taxable benefit on acquisitions is restricted to current market value, minus the price paid by the employee. To the extent that the £500 limit for computer equipment has not been used up by the annual use charge for the tax year, the excess can be deducted from this charge.

Rupert is provided with a new laptop computer by his employer on 6 April 2005. The computer is available for private use. It cost the employer £1,500 when new. On 6 October 2005 the employer transfers ownership of the laptop to Rupert when it is worth £800. Rupert does not pay anything for the computer.

What is the total taxable benefit on Rupert for 2005/06 in respect of the computer?

student notes

Solution

	£
Use benefit £1,500 × 20% × 6/12	150
Less: exemption	(150)
Taxable benefit	NIL

Transfer benefit (use MV at acquisition by employee only)

	£
MV at transfer	800
Less: balance of exemption £(500 - 150)	(350)
Taxable benefit	450

Beneficial loans

Employer loans give rise to a benefit equal to:

a) any amounts written off; and

b) the excess of the official rate of interest on the loan over any interest actually charged.

Calculating the interest benefit

There are two methods of calculating the interest benefit. The 'average' method applies automatically unless an election is made by the taxpayer or the Revenue. (The Revenue normally only make the election where it appears that the 'average' method is being deliberately exploited.)

The first method averages the balance of the loan at the beginning and end of the tax year (or the dates on which the loan was made and discharged if it was not in existence throughout the year) and applies the official rate of interest to this average. If the loan was not in existence throughout the year only the number of complete tax months (from the 6th of the month) for which it existed are taken into account.

The second method is to compute interest at the official rate on a daily basis on the actual amount outstanding.

How it works

At 6 April 2005 a low interest loan of £30,000 was outstanding to a director, who repaid £20,000 on 6 December 2005. The remaining balance of £10,000 was outstanding at 5 April 2006. Interest paid during the year was £250.

student notes

What is the benefit under both methods for 2005/06, assuming that the official rate of interest was 5% throughout 2005/06.

Solution

Average method

	£
$5\% \times \dfrac{(30{,}000 + 10{,}000)}{2}$	1,000
Less: interest paid	(250)
Taxable benefit	750

Alternative method

	£
£30,000 × 8/12 (6 April 2005 – 5 December 2005) × 5%	1,000
£10,000 × 4/12 (6 December 2005 – 5 April 2006) × 5%	167
	1,167
Less: interest paid	(250)
Taxable benefit	917

The de minimis test

No taxable benefit arises if the total balance on all loans to the employee did not exceed £5,000 at any time in the year.

When the £5,000 threshold is exceeded, a benefit arises on interest on the whole loan, not just on the excess of the loan over £5,000.

When a loan is written off and a benefit arises, there is no £5,000 threshold: writing off a loan of £1 gives rise to a £1 benefit.

How it works

Annika, has two loans from her employer:

a) A season ticket loan of £2,300 at no interest

b) A loan of £24,000 at 2% interest which Annika used to buy a holiday cottage

The official rate of interest is 5%.

What taxable benefit arises in respect of the loans in 2005/06?

student notes

Solution

As the total of the loans exceeds £5,000 a taxable benefit arises in respect of both loans.

	£
£2,300 × 5%	115
£24,000 × (5% – 2%)	720
	835

Activity 5

On 6 April 2005 Anton's employer provided him with an interest free season ticket loan of £6,200. He repaid £1,000 of this loan on 6 October 2005. The official rate of interest is 5%. Calculate the taxable benefit arising in respect of the loan assuming no elections are made.

Expenses connected with living accommodation

The following living expenses incurred in connection with living accommodation give rise to a taxable benefit:

a) heating, lighting or cleaning the premises;

b) repairing, maintaining or decorating them;

c) providing furniture etc. normal for domestic occupation (annual value taken as 20% of cost).

If the accommodation is job-related (see below), the maximum chargeable benefit in respect of the above expenses is 10% of the employee's net earnings.

EXEMPT BENEFITS

There is a fairly long list of benefits that are not taxable on any employees, including:

a) **Accommodation and subsistence**

Living accommodation which constitutes job-related accommodation. Accommodation is job related if:

i) residence in the accommodation is necessary for the proper performance of the employee's duties (eg a caretaker); or

student notes

iii) accommodation is provided for the better performance of the employee's duties and the employment is of a kind in which it is customary for accommodation to be provided (eg a vicar or policeman); or

iii) the accommodation is provided as part of special security arrangements in force because of a special threat to the employee's security (eg the Prime Minister).

b) **Subsistence**

i) Meals in a staff canteen, if they are available to all employees on broadly similar terms.

ii) The first 15p per working day of meal vouchers.

iii) Personal incidental expenses of up to £5 per night for employees working away from home in the UK, or £10 per night if working abroad which would otherwise be taxable. (eg laundry, newspapers, telephone calls home).

However, where more than one night is spent away, the exemption works on an aggregate basis eg for four nights the overall limit is £20.

c) **Travel**

(i) The provision of a parking space at or near the place of work.

ii) Mileage allowances for cars, motor bikes and bicycles within the statutory limits (see above).

iii) The provision of works buses with a seating capacity of 9 or more which are used mainly to bring employees to and from work.

iv) The payment of general subsidies to public bus services used by employees to travel to work.

v) The provision of bicycles and cycling safety equipment made available for employees mainly to travel between home and work.

vi) Tax free breakfasts on official cycle to work days.

d) Removal expenses: up to £8,000 of removal expenses borne by the employer where the employee has to move house on first taking up the employment or on a transfer within the organisation.

e) Entertainment: the provision of staff parties provided that the cost is no more than £150 per head per annum.

f) Child care: The cost of running a workplace nursery or play scheme (without limit). Otherwise up to £50 a week is tax free if the employer contracts with an approved child carer or provides child

student notes

care vouchers to pay an approved child carer. The childcare must be available to all employees and the childcare must be registered or approved home child care.

g) Home-working: A tax free allowance of up to £104 pa is payable to employees to cover the additional household costs of working some or all of the time at home. No record keeping is required for the flat-rate £104 allowance. For payments above that figure, evidence will be required that the payment is wholly in respect of additional household expenses incurred by the employee in carrying out his duties at home.

h) **Miscellaneous**

   i) Non-cash long service awards – for service in excess of 20 years, £50 per year of service is tax-free.

   ii) Awards under a formally constituted staff suggestion scheme.

   iii) Workplace sports or recreational facilities provided by employers for use by their staff generally. This does not apply where the employer pays or reimburses an employee's subscription to a sports club nor where the facilities are only available to limited groups of employees.

   iv) Air miles obtained in the course of business travel.

CHAPTER OVERVIEW

> **KEY WORDS**
>
> **Excluded employees** are employees who are not directors and who earn at the rate of less than £8,500 per annum
>
> **Second hand value** is the amount a benefit would fetch if the employee disposed of it to a third party
>
> **Job related accommodation** is accommodation that is either necessary for the proper performance of duties, is customarily provided, or is provided as part of special security arrangements

- It is important to distinguish between an employment (assessable as employment income) and self-employment (assessable as business profits). The basic question is whether the person is employed under a contract of service, or performs services under a contract for services and is therefore self-employed
- An employee's earnings comprise not only his wages or salary but also employer provided benefits
- The charge to tax on employer provided benefits varies according to whether the individual is an excluded employee or not
- In relation to excluded employees, the general rule is that the value of any benefit provided is the second-hand value, ie the amount of money into which it can be converted. The charge is extended in the case of the employees paid £8,500 + and directors. In this case the general rule is that the benefit is equal to the cost of providing the benefit
- The provision of living accommodation (unless it is job-related accommodation), credit cards, cash or non-cash vouchers, and mileage allowances in excess of the statutory mileage rates gives rise to a taxable benefit, for all employees
- The living accommodation benefit is based on the rental value of the property. An additional benefit arises where the cost of the property, or in certain circumstances the market value at the date it is first occupied, exceeds £75,000
- The benefits which are chargeable on employees paid £8,500+ and on directors by reference to special rules are: use of assets owned by the employer; the provision of a company car and of petrol for private mileage; the provision of a company van with private use and cheap or interest-free loans
- Expenses incurred by the employer in connection with the provision of living accommodation are fully assessable on the employee/director, unless the employee/ director is in job related accommodation. In the latter case, the maximum benefit is 10% of the net earnings from the employment
- There are certain benefits which are not taxable on any employees (eg. the provision of meals in a staff canteen)
- For employment related expenses to be deductible such expenses must be 'wholly, exclusively and necessarily' incurred 'in the performance of' the employee's duties.
- Employees generally are allowed a deduction for travel costs incurred in the performance of their duties or incurred in travelling to and from a temporary workplace. Temporary is taken to be not exceeding 24 months.
- A deduction from taxable earnings is given to employees for the cost of using their own vehicle for business travel if any mileage allowance paid is less than the statutory rates. Any excess is taxable.

HOW MUCH HAVE YOU LEARNED?

1 Someone is regarded as self-employed if he has a contract ...., whereas if he has a contract ...., he will be regarded as an employee. Fill in the missing words.

2 Expenses are deductible in computing taxable earnings if they are incurred ...., ... and .... in the performance of the duties of employment. Fill in the missing words.

3 Brian uses his own car to travel 8,000 business miles in 2005/06. Brian's employer reimburses him with 35p per mile travelled. The statutory mileage rates for the first 10,000 business miles travelled is 40p per mile. What amounts are taxable/deductible in calculating employment income?

4 An employee is provided with a flat by his employer (not job-related accommodation). The annual value of the flat is £400; rent paid by the employer amounts to £3,900 per annum.

What is the taxable value of this benefit?

5 The additional charge on 'expensive' accommodation (costing more than £75,000) applies only to employees who are not excluded employees. TRUE/FALSE?

6 Is a taxable fuel benefit reduced by any reimbursement by the employee of the cost of fuel provided for private mileage?

7 A video recorder costing £500 was made available to Gordon by his employer on 6 April 2004. On 6 April 2005, Gordon bought the recorder for £150, when its market value was £325. What assessable benefit arises in 2005/06 if Gordon's salary amounts to £15,000 per annum?

8 The first £5,000 of an interest-free loan is exempt from tax. TRUE/FALSE?

9 Gautown was supplied with a petrol engined car by his employer throughout 2005/06. The list price of the car was £24,000 and its CO_2 emissions are 187 g/km. What taxable benefit arises in respect of the car?

10 Buster is the Managing Director of Buster Braces Ltd and is supplied with a Bentley (3 litre, petrol engine) which cost £82,000. It has CO_2 emissions of 200g/km. The car is fitted with a telephone which Buster uses both for business and privately. All running costs are borne by the company. What is the total taxable benefit?

chapter 4: EMPLOYMENT INCOME – ADDITIONAL ASPECTS

chapter coverage

In this chapter you will continue your studies of the calculation of employment income.

We begin by learning how payments made on the termination of employment are taxed. We then learn when tax relief is available for pension contributions.

Finally we consider how tax is deducted at source from employment income under the PAYE system and we look at various forms that must be completed either by the employer or by the taxpayer.

The topics that we shall cover are:

- The termination of employment
- Pensions
- The PAYE system
- Forms

KNOWLEDGE AND UNDERSTANDING AND PERFORMANCE CRITERIA COVERAGE

knowledge and understanding

- The issues of taxation liability (Elements 19.1, 19.2, 19.3, 19.4)
- Basic law and practice (Elements 19.1, 19.2, 19.3, 19.4)
- Expenses deductible from employment income including pension contributions and payroll giving to charities (Element 19.1)

Performance criteria

- List allowable expenses and deductions
- Record relevant details of income from employment accurately and legibly in the tax return
- Make computations and submissions in accordance with current tax law and taking account of current Revenue practice

student notes

THE TERMINATION OF EMPLOYMENT

Payments made on the termination of employment are either:

a) entirely exempt; or
b) partially exempt; or
c) entirely chargeable.

The following are exempt:

a) payments made on death;
b) payments made on account of injury or disability;
c) a lump sum payment from an approved pension scheme;

Termination packages made in return for services are fully taxable. This includes all benefits to which an employee is contractually entitled, such as payment of salary in lieu of notice.

Other termination packages are PARTIALLY EXEMPT TERMINATION PACKAGES. This includes ex-gratia payments and statutory redundancy pay. The first £30,000 of any such package is exempt. Any amount in excess of £30,000 is taxable.

Payments and benefits received on termination of employment are taxable in the year in which they are received or enjoyed, rather than being taxed in the year of termination. Similarly any benefits (eg the provision of a company car) which would be taxable had the employment continued, are taxed in the year in which the benefit is received or enjoyed.

If the termination package is a partially exempt one and exceeds £30,000 then the £30,000 exempt limit is allocated to earlier benefits and payments.

How it works

Jonty is made redundant on 31 March 2006. He receives the following redundancy package:

- cash of £10,000 payable on 31 March 2006 and £40,000 payable in September 2006
- use of company car for period to 30 September 2006 (benefit value per annum £5,000)

The redundancy package is a partially exempt one. Show the amounts taxable on Jonty and the tax year in which they are taxed.

student notes

Solution

In 2005/06 Jonty receives as redundancy:

	£
Cash	10,000

This is wholly exempt as it falls within the first £30,000 of a partially exempt payment.

In 2006/07 Jonty receives:

	£
Cash	40,000
Car (6/12)	2,500
	42,500
Exemption (remaining)	(20,000)
Taxable in 2006/07	22,500

Activity 1

Chan is made redundant on 30 June 2005. She receives the following redundancy package:

Ex-gratia cash payment paid 30 June 2005 = £28,000

Use of her company car until 30 December 2005 (Annual benefit value – £8,800)

There is no contractual obligation for Chan's employer to provide either of these items.

What amount, if any, of the above redundancy package is taxable in 2005/06?

PENSIONS

The main ways in which individuals can provide for a pension are:

a) the state pension scheme;
b) occupational pension schemes;
c) personal pension schemes.

The state scheme has no impact on income tax during an individual's working career, but the other schemes are discussed below.

student notes

Occupational pension schemes

An occupational pension scheme is an employer run pension scheme. A scheme may be a Revenue approved scheme or an unapproved scheme. Approved schemes have significant tax advantages:

(a) An employee can deduct his contributions from his employment income (up to a limit of 15% of gross earnings, with gross earnings limited to an EARNINGS CAP of £105,600 for 2005/06)

(b) Employer contributions are not taxable benefits for the employee

(c) Provision can be made for a tax-free lump sum to be paid on the employee's retirement or death in service

Activity 2

The managing director of Bus Ltd will receive a salary of £120,000 in 2005/06. What is the maximum amount that the managing director can pay into the company's occupational pension scheme in 2005/06?

Additional voluntary contributions

An employee who feels that his employer's scheme is inadequate may make additional voluntary contributions (AVCs), either to the employer's scheme or to a separate scheme (freestanding AVCs).

AVCs are deductible from the employee's taxable earnings, but only to the extent that they, plus any contributions by the employee to the employer's scheme, do not exceed 15% of gross earnings (limited to the earnings cap).

Freestanding AVCs are paid net of 22% tax.

Benefits

The maximum benefits that can be taken from an occupational pension scheme are:

a) a pension equal to 2/3 final remuneration
b) a tax free lump sum equal to $1\frac{1}{2} \times$ final remuneration.

For these purposes final remuneration cannot exceed the earnings cap.

Personal pension schemes (PPS) – stakeholder pensions

student notes

Broadly, any individual who is not a member of an occupational pension scheme can set up a personal pension scheme (PPS). You may sometimes see a personal pension scheme referred to as a stakeholder scheme.

Contributions

All individuals can pay contributions of up to £3,600 pa. In certain circumstances an individual may pay contributions in excess of the contributions threshold. In the exam you will always be told the amount of pension contribution paid.

Contributions are paid net of 22% tax (so all individuals obtain at least 22% tax relief). Higher rate tax relief is obtained by increasing the payer's basic rate tax band by the amount of the gross contribution (see chapter 2).

THE PAYE SYSTEM

The Pay As You Earn method of deducting income tax from salaries and wages applies to all income from offices or employments.

It is the employer's duty to deduct income tax and national insurance from the pay of his employees, whether or not he has been directed to do so by the Revenue. If he fails to do this he may be required to pay over the tax that he should have deducted and, in addition, may be subject to penalties.

Employers are required to pay PAYE deductions made on paydays falling between 6th of a calendar month and 5th of the next calendar month to the Collector within 14 days of the end of the tax month. For example, PAYE deducted on a 24 September 2005 pay day must be paid by 19 October 2005. However, for employers whose monthly payments of PAYE and NIC are less than £1,500 on average, payments can be made quarterly. Payments for quarters ending 5 July, 5 October, 5 January, and 5 April will be due on the 19th day of those months.

Charitable donations under payroll deduction scheme

If an employer has set up a payroll deduction scheme, employees within the PAYE system can make tax deductible donations to an approved charity of their choice by asking the employer to deduct a donation from their gross earnings before calculating PAYE.

student notes

Employees joining or leaving

When an employee leaves, a Form P45 (Particulars of employee leaving) must be prepared. This shows details of income and tax paid to the date of leaving. This form is prepared in four parts. Part 1 must be sent to the Revenue. The other three parts are given to the employee leaving. The employee will keep part 1A for his own records and hand parts 2 and 3 to his new employer.

End of year returns

At the end of each tax year the employer must complete a number of forms as detailed in the table below.

Form	Content	Due date
P35	Summary of tax and NIC deducted in the year	Provide to Revenue by 19 May following tax year
P14	Tax and NIC for each employee (same details as on P60 provided to each employee)	Provide to Revenue by 19 May following tax year
P11D	Benefits and reimbursed expenses for all employees paid £8,500 pa or more	Provide to Revenue and employee by 6 July following tax year
P9D	Benefits and expense payments to excluded employees	Provide to Revenue and employee by 6 July following tax year
P60	For each employee, total earnings and tax for the year	Provide to employee by 31 May following tax year

FORMS

In your exam you may have to complete the supplementary employment pages that accompany the income tax return form. We have included a sample of these pages at the end of this chapter. Have a look at them now. You will be able to practice using this form in the practice exams later in this Course Companion.

In addition you may, in your exam, be required to take information from either forms P60 or P11D. You will not be required to complete these forms. We have included a sample of these pages at the end of this chapter, so that you can familiarise yourself with the information contained on them.

student notes

You can see that you may need to take details of pay and tax deducted from Form P60. Form P11D contains details of the taxable value of various benefits.

See page (v) for a note regarding these forms.

CHAPTER OVERVIEW

- The first £30,000 of an ex gratia termination payment is exempt from tax, the remainder of the payment is fully taxable
- Any termination payment to which an employee is contractually entitled is fully taxable
- Termination payments are taxed in the year in which they are received

KEY WORDS

Partially exempt termination packages are packages where the first £30,000 is exempt from income tax.

The **earnings cap** is the maximum level of earnings on which pension contributions may be based

- Occupational pension schemes are employer run schemes. Contributions of up to 15% of earnings can be made to these schemes (subject to the earnings cap of £105,600 in 2005/06).
- Contributions to an occupational pension scheme are deducted from the employee's taxable earnings.
- Any individual who is not a member of occupation pension scheme can pay up to £3,600 to a Personal Pension Scheme (PPS). In certain circumstances additional contributions can be paid.
- Basic rate tax relief is given by treating personal pension contributions as having been made net of 22% tax. Additional tax relief is given by extending the basic rate band
- PAYE is the method employers use for deducting income tax and national insurance from salaries and wages
- When an employee leaves a P45 must be given to him. He must provide two parts of the form to his new employer
- The employer must complete various end of year returns (P60, P35, P14, P11D, P9D)
- Employees can make charitable donations under an employer's payroll deduction scheme. Such payments are deductible in arriving at taxable earnings

HOW MUCH HAVE YOU LEARNED?

1 In the case where an employer sets up a Revenue – approved pension scheme, up to ....% of the employee's earnings may be contributed to the scheme and can be deducted in computing ....

Fill in the blanks.

2 How do individuals obtain tax relief for personal pension contributions?

3 Which form is given to an employee when leaving an employment?

4 What is a form P11D used for? By what date must this form be submitted to the Revenue?

5 Sandy is made redundant on 31 March 2006. On 30 June 2006 her employer paid her an ex-gratia redundancy payment of £35,000. What amount, if any, of this payment is taxable and in which tax year?

Income for the year ended 5 April 2006

EMPLOYMENT

Fill in these boxes first

Name	Tax reference

If you want help, look up the box numbers in the Notes.

Details of employer

Employer's PAYE reference - may be shown under 'Revenue and Customs office number and reference' on your P60 or 'PAYE reference' on your P45

1.1

Employer's name

1.2

Date employment started (only if between 6 April 2005 and 5 April 2006)

1.3 / /

Date employment finished (only if between 6 April 2005 and 5 April 2006)

1.4 / /

Tick box 1.6 if you were a director of the company

1.6

and, if so, tick box 1.7 if it was a close company

1.7

Employer's address

1.5

Postcode

Income from employment

■ ***Money*** *- see Notes, page EN3.*

		Before tax
• Payments from P60 (or P45)		1.8 £
• Payments not on P60, etc.	- tips	1.9 £
	- other payments (excluding expenses entered below and lump sums and compensation payments or benefits entered overleaf)	1.10 £

	Tax taken off
• UK tax taken off payments in boxes 1.8 to 1.10	1.11 £

■ ***Benefits and expenses*** *- see Notes, pages EN3 to EN6. If any benefits connected with termination of employment were received, or enjoyed, after that termination and were from a* ***former*** *employer you need to complete Help Sheet IR204, available from the Orderline. Do not enter such benefits here.*

	Amount		Amount
• Assets transferred/ payments made for you	1.12 £	• Vans	1.18 £
• Vouchers, credit cards and tokens	1.13 £	• Interest-free and low-interest loans *see Note for box 1.19, page EN5.*	1.19 £
• Living accommodation	1.14 £	*box 1.20 is not used.*	
• Excess mileage allowance and passenger payments	1.15 £	• Private medical or dental insurance	1.21 £
• Company cars	1.16 £	• Other benefits	1.22 £
• Fuel for company cars	1.17 £	• Expenses payments received and balancing charges	1.23 £

SA101

BS 12/04net — TAX RETURN ■ EMPLOYMENT: PAGE E1 — *Please turn over*

Income from employment continued

■ ***Lump sums and compensation payments or benefits including such payments and benefits from a former employer***
Note that 'lump sums' here includes any contributions which your employer made to an unapproved retirement benefits scheme.

You must read page EN6 of the Notes before filling in boxes 1.24 to 1.30.

Reliefs

- £30,000 exception — 1.24 £
- Foreign service and disability — 1.25 £
- Retirement and death lump sums — 1.26 £

Taxable lump sums

- From box B of *Help Sheet IR204* — 1.27 £
- From box K of *Help Sheet IR204* — 1.28 £
- From box L of *Help Sheet IR204* — 1.29 £
- Tax taken off payments in boxes 1.27 to 1.29 - *leave blank if this tax is included in the box 1.11 figure and tick box 1.30A.* — Tax taken off 1.30 £
- Tick this box if you have left box 1.30 blank because the tax is included in the box 1.11 figure — 1.30A

■ ***Foreign earnings not taxable in the UK in the year ended 5 April 2006*** *- see Notes, pages EN6 to EN7* — 1.31 £

■ ***Expenses you incurred in doing your job*** *- see Notes, pages EN7 to EN8.*

- Travel and subsistence costs — 1.32 £
- Fixed deductions for expenses — 1.33 £
- Professional fees and subscriptions — 1.34 £
- Other expenses and capital allowances — 1.35 £
- Tick box 1.36 if the figure in box 1.32 includes travel between your home and a permanent workplace — 1.36

■ ***Seafarers' Earnings Deduction*** *(enter the amount of the earnings that attract the deduction, not the tax)* — 1.37 £

■ ***Foreign tax for which tax credit relief not claimed*** — 1.38 £

Student Loans

■ ***Student Loans repaid by deduction by employer*** *- see Notes, page EN8* — 1.39 £

- Tick box 1.39A if your income is under Repayment of Teachers' Loans Scheme — 1.39A

1.40 ***Additional information***

Now fill in any other supplementary Pages that apply to you.
Otherwise, go back to page 2 in your Tax Return and finish filling it in.

Do not destroy — **P60 End of Year Certificate 2005-06**

Your employer's name and address

Inland Revenue office name

Employer's PAYE reference /

For employer's use

Tax Year to 5 April **2 0 0 6**

Your private address

To the employee:
Please keep this certificate in a safe place as **you will need it if you have to fill in a Tax Return or make a claim for Tax Credits.** It also helps you check that your employer is using the correct National Insurance number and deducting the right rate of National Insurance contributions. **By law you are required to tell the Inland Revenue about any income that is not fully taxed, even if you are not sent a Tax Return.**
INLAND REVENUE

Your details

National Insurance number

Sex 'M' – male, 'F' – female

Surname

First two forenames

Works/payroll no. etc

Please tell your Inland Revenue office and employer if there are any changes to your personal details, for example your address

National Insurance contributions in this employment *(Note: LEL = Lower Earnings Limit, ET = Earnings Threshold, UEL = Upper Earnings Limit)*

NIC table letter	Earnings at the LEL (where earnings are equal to or exceed the LEL) *(whole £s only)* £	Earnings above the LEL, up to and including the ET *(whole £s only)* £	Earnings above the ET, up to and including the UEL *(whole £s only)* £	Employee's contributions £ p	Scheme Contracted-out Number *(For Contracted-out Money Purchase schemes OR Contracted-out Money Purchase Stakeholder Pension schemes only)*
				•	S
				•	S
				•	S
				•	S

Statutory payments included in the pay 'In this employment' figure below

Statutory Maternity Pay £ p	Statutory Paternity Pay £ p	Statutory Adoption Pay £ p
•	•	•

Certificate by Employer/Paying Office:

This form shows your total pay for Income Tax purposes in this employment for the year. Any overtime, bonus, commission etc, Statutory Sick Pay, Statutory Maternity Pay, Statutory Paternity Pay and Statutory Adoption Pay is included.

Pay and Income Tax details	Pay £ p	Tax deducted £ p
In previous employment(s)	•	
★ In this employment	•	Enter 'R' in this box if net refund
Total for year	•	

Employee's Widows & Orphans/Life Assurance contributions in this employment ★ £ p

Final tax code

Student Loan Deductions in this employment *(whole £s only)* £

Tax Credits in this employment £ p

The figures aside marked ★ should be used for your Tax Return, if you get one

Week 53 payment indicator

BS11/04

P60 (2005-06)

Inland Revenue

P11D EXPENSES AND BENEFITS 2005-06

Note to employer
Complete this return for a director, or an employee who earned at a rate of £8,500 a year or more during the year 6 April 2005 to 5 April 2006. Do not include expenses and benefits covered by a dispensation or PAYE settlement agreement. Read the P11D Guide and Booklet 480, Chapter 24, before you complete the form. You must give a copy of this information to the director or employee by 6 July 2006. The term employee is used to cover both directors and employees throughout the rest of this form. **Send the completed P11D and form P11D(b) to the Inland Revenue office by 6 July 2006.**

Note to employee
Your employer has filled in this form. Keep it in a safe place as you may not be able to get a duplicate. You will need it for your tax records and to complete your 2004-05 Tax Return if you get one. Your tax code may need to be adjusted to take account of the information given on this P11D. The box numbers on this P11D have the same numbering as the Employment Pages of the Tax Return, for example, 1.12. Include the total figures in the corresponding box on the Tax Return, unless you think some other figure is more appropriate.

Employer's details
Employer's name
Employer's PAYE reference

Employee's details
Employee's name — If a director tick here
Works number /department — National Insurance number

Employers pay Class 1A National Insurance contributions on most benefits. These are shown in boxes which are brown and have a 1A indicator

A Assets transferred (cars, property, goods or other assets)

	Cost/ Market value		Amount made good or from which tax deducted		Cash equivalent
Description of asset	£	–	£	=	1.12 £ 1A

B Payments made on behalf of employee

Description of payment — 1.12 £

Tax on notional payments not borne by employee within 90 days of receipt of each notional payment — 1.12 £

C Vouchers or credit cards

	Gross amount		Amount made good or from which tax deducted		Cash equivalent
Value of vouchers and payments made using credit cards or tokens	£	–	£	=	1.13 £

D Living accommodation

Cash equivalent of accommodation provided for employee, or his/ her family or household — Cash equivalent 1.14 £ 1A

E Mileage allowance and passenger payments

Amount of car and mileage allowances paid to employee for business travel in employee's own vehicle, and passenger payments, in excess of maximum exempt amounts *(See P11D Guide for 2005-06 exempt rates)* — Taxable amount 1.15 £

F Cars and car fuel *If more than two cars were made available, either at the same time or in succession, please give details on a separate sheet*

	Car 1	Car 2
Make and Model		
Date first registered	/ /	/ /
Approved CO2 emissions figure for cars registered on or after 1 January 1998 *Tick box if the car does not have an approved CO2 figure*	g/km ☐ *See P11D Guide for details of cars that have no approved CO2 figure*	g/km ☐ *See P11D Guide for details of cars that have no approved CO2 figure*
Engine size	cc	cc
Type of fuel or power used *Please use the key letter shown in the P11D Guide (2005)*		
Dates car was available *Only enter a 'from' or 'to' date if the car was first made available and/or ceased to be available in 2004-05*	From / / to / /	From / / to / /
List price of car *Including car and standard accessories only: if there is no list price, or if it is a classic car, employers see booklet 480; employees see leaflet IR172*	£	£
Accessories *All non-standard accessories, see P11D Guide*	£	£
Capital contributions (maximum £5,000) the employee made towards the cost of car or accessories	£	£
Amount paid by employee for private use of the car	£	£
Date free fuel was withdrawn *Tick if reinstated in year (see P11D Guide)*	/ / ☐	/ / ☐
Cash equivalent of each car	£	£

Total cash equivalent of all cars available in 2005-06 — 1.16 £ 1A

	Car 1	Car 2
Cash equivalent of fuel for each car	£	£

Total cash equivalent of fuel for all cars available in 2005-06 — 1.17 £ 1A

P11D(2005) BS 09/04

G Vans

Cash equivalent of all vans made available for private use	1.18 £	1A

H Interest-free and low interest loans

If the total amount outstanding on all loans does not exceed £5,000 at any time in the year, there is no need for details in this section.

	Loan 1	Loan 2
Number of joint borrowers *(if applicable)*		
Amount outstanding at 5 April 2005 or at date loan was made if later	£	£
Amount outstanding at 5 April 2006 or at date loan was discharged if earlier	£	£
Maximum amount outstanding at any time in the year	£	£
Total amount of interest paid by the borrower in 2005-06– *enter "NIL" if none was paid*	£	£
Date loan was made in 2005-06 if applicable	/ /	/ /
Date loan was discharged in 2005-06 if applicable	/ /	/ /
Cash equivalent of loans after deducting any interest paid by the borrower	1.19 £ 1A	1.19 £ 1A

I Private medical treatment or insurance

	Cost to you		Amount made good or from which tax deducted		Cash equivalent
Private medical treatment or insurance	£	–	£	=	1.21 £ 1A

J Qualifying relocation expenses payments and benefits

Non-qualifying benefits and expenses go in sections M and N below

Excess over £8,000 of all qualifying relocation expenses payments and benefits for each move	1.22 £ 1A

K Services supplied

	Cost to you		Amount made good or from which tax deducted		Cash equivalent
Services supplied to the employee	£	–	£	=	1.22 £ 1A

L Assets placed at the employee's disposal

		Annual value plus expenses incurred		Amount made good or from which tax deducted		Cash equivalent
Description of asset		£	–	£	=	1.22 £ 1A

M Other items (including subscriptions and professional fees)

		Cost to you		Amount made good or from which tax deducted		Cash equivalent
Description of other items		£	–	£	=	1.22 £ 1A
Description of other items		£	–	£	=	1.22 £

	Tax paid
Income tax paid but not deducted from director's remuneration	1.22 £

N Expenses payments made to, or on behalf of, the employee

		Cost to you		Amount made good or from which tax deducted		Taxable payment
Travelling and subsistence payments (except mileage allowance payments for employee's own car - *see section E*)		£	–	£	=	1.23 £
Entertainment *(trading organisations read P11D Guide and then enter a tick or a cross as appropriate here)*	☐	£	–	£	=	1.23 £
General expenses allowance for business travel		£	–	£	=	1.23 £
Payments for use of home telephone		£	–	£	=	1.23 £
Non-qualifying relocation expenses *(those not shown in sections J or M)*		£	–	£	=	1.23 £
Description of other expenses		£	–	£	=	1.23 £

chapter 5: PROPERTY INCOME

chapter coverage

In this chapter we will see how to compute the net rental income that an individual landlord is taxed on in a tax year. We will then look at the special rules that apply for furnished holiday lettings.

We end the chapter by looking at the supplementary land and property pages that must accompany the income tax return form of an individual who has let property in the tax year concerned.

The topics that we shall cover are:

- Computing net rental income
- Furnished holiday lettings
- Land and Property tax form pages

KNOWLEDGE AND UNDERSTANDING AND PERFORMANCE CRITERIA COVERAGE

knowledge and understanding

- The issues of taxation liability (Elements 19.1, 19.2, 19.3, 19.4)
- Basic law and practice (Elements 19.1, 19.2, 19.3, 19.4)
- Classification and calculation of income as property income, savings or dividend income (Element 19.2)
- Calculation and set off of rental deficits (element 19.2)

Performance criteria

- Prepare schedules of property income and determine profits and losses
- Apply deductions and reliefs and claim loss set-offs
- Record relevant details of property and investment income accurately and legibly in the tax return

student notes

COMPUTING NET RENTAL INCOME

For individual landlords, rental income is taxed as non-savings income on an ACCRUALS BASIS. This means that all rental income accruing in a tax year is taxed in that year.

How it works

Susi bought a property on 30 September 2005. Susi began letting the property immediately for an annual rent of £36,000 payable in advance in monthly instalments on the first day of each month. How much rental income is Susi taxed on in 2005/06?

Solution

Rental income is taxed on an accruals basis. This means the income for the period between 30 September 2005 and 5 April 2006. In 2005/06 Susi is therefore taxed on £36,000 × 6/12 = £18,000. The date the rental income is received is not relevant for tax purposes.

Expenses are allowed on an accruals basis if they are revenue expenses wholly and exclusively incurred for the purpose of letting. Common deductible expenses include:

a) advertising, accountancy and insurance

b) bad debts if a rent payment appears unlikely

c) management and agents fees

d) maintenance and repair costs, but not the costs of improvements. For example the cost of replacing some broken tiles on a roof is a repair, but the cost of replacing the whole roof is not.

e) loan interest and overdraft interest if the related borrowing was applied wholly and exclusively for the purposes of letting properties.

How it works

Nadine has let a property unfurnished for many years. She charged rental income of £40,000 for the year to 31 December 2005. The annual rent rose to £44,000 with effect from 1 January 2006.

student notes

Expenses relating to the letting were:

	£
Water rates (year to 31 March 2006)	2,000
Insurance (year to 31 December 2005)	600
Insurance (year to 31 December 2006)	800

Agents fees – 10% of rental income

In June 2005 the tenant accidentally flooded the bathroom. Nadine took the opportunity to refurbish the whole bathroom at a total cost of £5,000. This included £900 that was the cost of repairing the flood damage.

On what amount of net rental income is Nadine taxable in 2005/06?

Solution

	£	£
Rental income		
(£40,000 × 9/12 + £44,000 × 3/12)		41,000
Less: water rates	2,000	
insurance (£600 × 9/12 + £800 × 3/12)	650	
agents fees	4,100	
repairs	900	
		(7,650)
		33,350

Notes

The rental income and expenses must be dealt with on an accruals basis.

The cost of the flood repairs is deductible. However, the cost of refurbishing the bathroom is not deductible.

Activity 1

Harry owns a property that is let for ten weeks from 1 July 2005 at a rent of £160 per week. The tenants leave at the end of this period having paid only £1,300 of the total amount due. Harry writes off the outstanding debt.

The property is re-let to new tenants on 1 March 2006 for a rent of £400 per month payable in arrears (that means at the end of the month). He received the first payment on 10 April 2006.

He paid interest of £700 during the year ended 5 April 2006 on a loan to purchase the property.

What is his Harry's taxable rental income for 2005/06?

student notes

All letting by an individual landlord is treated as a single source of income. This means that rents and expenses accruing in a tax year on all let properties must be pooled to arrive at a single figure for net rental income. If the landlord lets several properties he can set-off the running expenses incurred on empty properties (eg properties under repair between lets), against property income generally.

How it works

Bahrat lets two properties in 2005/06 as follows:

Property 1 was bought in June 2005 and let from 1 July 2005 at an annual rent of £18,000 per annum. Buildings insurance of £8,000 was paid for the year to 30 June 2006. £1,200 was spent in May 2005 on advertising for tenants.

Property 2 became vacant on 1 April 2005. Bahrat then spent £5,000 on repairing the leaking roof in the property. The property was let again with effect from 1 March 2006 for £24,000 per annum payable monthly in advance. Buildings insurance of £1,800 was incurred for the year to 31 March 2006.

Calculate Bahrat's net rental income for 2005/06.

Solution

	£	£
Rental income – property one		
(9/12 × £18,000)		13,500
Rental income – property two		
(£24,000 × 1/12)		2,000
Less: buildings insurance (9/12 × £8,000)	6,000	
advertising for tenants	1,200	
repairs	5,000	
buildings insurance	1,800	
		(14,000)
Net rental income		1,500

Note that a loss would have arisen on property two if it had been dealt with separately. Pooling income and expenses on all let properties allows a loss on one property to be set against gains on other properties.

student notes

Activity 2

Johnson owns two properties:

Whitehouse – let at a rental of £14,000 per annum, payable quarterly in advance. The tenant was late in paying the last quarter's rent for the quarter to 5 April 2006 and Johnson did not receive payment until 25 April 2006.

Blackhouse – let at a rent of £6,800 per annum payable quarterly in advance. Blackhouse was unlet throughout 2004/05; however, a tenant moved in on 24 December 2005.

Johnson pays agents fees of 15% in respect of both properties to his managing agent. He has also incurred the following expenses:

	Whitehouse	*Blackhouse*
	£	£
Buildings insurance – year to 30 June 2005	1,200	980
– year to 30 June 2006	1,400	1,100
Advertising for tenants	–	450

What is Johnson's taxable rental income for 2005/06?

Depreciation on plant and machinery used in the letting business is never allowable as capital allowances (a form of depreciation for tax purposes) are given instead. In unit 19 you will never be expected to compute capital allowances but you may be given a figure for capital allowances that you are expected to deduct in computing the net rental income. You will learn how to compute capital allowance if you study Unit 18, Preparing Business Tax Computations.

Capital allowances are not allowed on furniture used in a dwelling. Instead, the Revenue gives relief for such capital expenditure on a RENEWALS BASIS. The original cost and the cost of any improvements are not relieved but the cost of replacing furniture to the same standard is allowed as an expense. As this is cumbersome to administer, a taxpayer can claim a WEAR AND TEAR ALLOWANCES instead. This allowance is equal to:

10% [rents – (water rates & council tax if paid by the landlord)]

and is allowed as a deduction in place of claiming relief for the replacement of furniture.

How it works

Polly lets out a furnished property for £8,000 per annum. She pays insurance of £300 per annum and water rates of £400 per annum. Polly chooses to claim the wear and tear allowance in respect of her furniture. What is the amount of Polly's net rental income for 2005/06?

student notes

Solution

	£	£
Rental income		8,000
Less insurance	300	
Water rates	400	
Wear and tear allowance		
(10% × £(8,000 – 400)	760	
		(1,460)
Net rental income		6,540

Activity 3

Sunita lets out a furnished property for £12,000 per annum. In 2005/06 she pays water rates of £800 and council tax of £900. She also pays an agents fee of 10% of rent to the agent who manages the letting.

Sunita chooses to claim the wear and tear allowance in respect of her furniture.

What is the amount of Sunita's net rental income for 2005/06?

Losses

If a landlord makes an overall loss from the letting of properties, the loss is carried forward and set against net rental income of the following year and subsequent years.

FURNISHED HOLIDAY LETTINGS

There are special rules for the taxation of income arising from furnished holiday lettings.

Provided certain conditions are satisfied the following special rules apply:

a) Losses can be set against other income in the tax year of the loss and/or in the preceding year.

b) The income qualifies as earnings for personal pension purposes. This means that it may be possible to pay premiums in excess of the contributions threshold (see earlier in this Course Companion).

c) Capital allowances are available on furniture. The renewals basis and the wear and tear allowance do not apply if capital allowances are given.

student notes

A FURNISHED HOLIDAY let is a letting of furnished accommodation made on a commercial basis with a view to the realisation of profit. The property must satisfy the following three conditions:

a) **The availability condition** – during the relevant period, the accommodation is available for **commercial let** as **holiday accommodation** to the **public** generally, for **at least 140 days**.

b) **The letting condition** – during the **relevant period**, the accommodation is **commercially let** as holiday accommodation to members of the public for at **least 70 days**. If the **landlord has more than one FHL**, at least one of which satisfies the 40 day rule ('qualifying holiday accommodation') and at least one of which does not, ('the underused accommodation') , he may elect to **average the occupation of the qualifying holiday accommodation, and any or all of the underused accommodation**. If the average of occupation is at least 70 days, the underused accommodation will be treated as qualifying holiday accommodation.

c) **The pattern of occupation condition** – during the **relevant period, not more that 155 days fall during periods of longer term occupation**. Longer term occupation is defined as **a continuous period of more than 31 days during which the accommodation is in the same occupation** unless there are abnormal circumstances.

The relevant period is normally the tax year. Where the FHL starts or ceases in a tax year, the relevant period is the 12 months beginning or ending with the first or last days of letting as appropriate.

Where the taxpayer also has other letting income, you must compute furnished holiday letting income separately.

LAND AND PROPERTY TAX FORM PAGES

In your exam you may be asked to complete the land and property pages that must accompany the income tax return of someone who lets property. A copy of these pages are included at the end of this chapter. Have a look at them now. You will be able to practise completing this form when you try the practice exams later in this Course Companion.

See page (v) of this Course Companion for a note regarding these forms.

CHAPTER OVERVIEW

- Net rental income accruing in a tax year is taxed in that year.
- If an individual lets more than one unfurnished property, the rents and expenses accruing on all of the let properties are pooled.
- A wear and tear allowance is available on furnished properties.
- Rental losses must be carried forward and set against future net rental profits.
- If a property meets various conditions it may be classified as a furnished holiday let (FHL).
- Losses form such furnished holiday lets can be set against other income in the year of the loss and/or in the preceding year.
- Income from furnished holiday lettings counts as net relevant earnings for pension purposes.

KEY WORDS

The **accruals basis** for taxing rental income means that all rent accruing in a tax year is taxed in that year

Under the **renewals basis** cost of replacing furniture is allowed as an expense

The **wear and tear allowance** is equal to 10% (rent – water rates – council tax paid by landlord). It may be claimed instead of the renewals basis

A **furnished holiday let** is a letting of furnished accommodation made on commercial terms with a view to realisation of profit for a certain time each year

HOW MUCH HAVE YOU LEARNED?

1 David buys a property for letting on 1 August 2005 and grants a tenancy to Ethel from 1 December 2005 at £3,600 pa. payable quarterly in advance. How much rental income is taxable in 2005/06?

2 Catherine rents out a furnished property for £16,000 pa. and pays the water rates of £320 and council tax of £780 on the property.

How will relief for wear and tear of furnishings be given?

3 John pays buildings insurance premiums for 12 months in advance on 1 October each year to cover all his letting properties. He pays £4,800 in 2004 and £5,200 in 2005.

How much would be allowed against his rental income for 2005/06?

4 Fred has let three holiday bungalows during 2005/06 making a net loss. Explain briefly the difference in treating this loss should the lettings count as furnished holiday lettings.

5 Where profits are being made what is the main income tax advantage of a 'furnished holiday letting' business?

6 Harry owns a property which he lets for the first time on 1 July 2005 at a rent of £4,000 per annum payable monthly in advance.

The first tenants left without notice on 28 February 2006 and the property was re-let to new tenants on 4 April 2006 at a rent of £5,000 per annum payable yearly in advance.

Harry's allowable expenditure was £1,000 in 2005/06.

What is his taxable rental income for 2005/06?

LAND AND PROPERTY

Name | **Tax reference**

Fill in these boxes first

If you want help, look up the box numbers in the Notes.

Are you claiming Rent a Room relief for gross rents of £4,250 or less?
(Or £2,125 if the claim is shared?)
Read the Notes on page LN2 to find out
- whether you can claim Rent a Room relief; and
- how to claim relief for gross rents over £4,250

Yes ☐ — If 'Yes', tick box. If this is your only income from UK property, you have finished these Pages

Is your income from furnished holiday lettings?
If not applicable, please turn over and fill in Page L2 to give details of your property income

Yes ☐ — If 'Yes', tick box and fill in boxes 5.1 to 5.18 before completing Page L2

Furnished holiday lettings

- **Income from furnished holiday lettings** — 5.1 £

■ ***Expenses*** (furnished holiday lettings only)

- Rent, rates, insurance, ground rents etc. — 5.2 £
- Repairs, maintenance and renewals — 5.3 £
- Finance charges, including interest — 5.4 £
- Legal and professional costs — 5.5 £
- Costs of services provided, including wages — 5.6 £
- Other expenses — 5.7 £ — total of boxes 5.2 to 5.7: 5.8 £

Net profit (put figures in brackets if a loss) — box 5.1 *minus* box 5.8: 5.9 £

■ ***Tax adjustments***

- Private use — 5.10 £
- Balancing charges — 5.11 £ — box 5.10 + box 5.11: 5.12 £
- Capital allowances — 5.13 £
- Tick box 5.13A if box 5.13 includes enhanced capital allowances for environmentally friendly expenditure — 5.13A ☐

Profit for the year (copy to box 5.19). If loss, enter '0' in box 5.14 and put the loss in box 5.15 — boxes 5.9 + 5.12 *minus* box 5.13: 5.14 £

Loss for the year (if you have entered '0' in box 5.14) — boxes 5.9 + 5.12 *minus* box 5.13: 5.15 £

■ ***Losses***

- Loss offset against 2005-06 total income — 5.16 £
- Loss - relief to be calculated by reference to earlier years — see Notes, page LN4: 5.17 £
- Loss offset against other income from property (copy to box 5.38) — see Notes, page LN4: 5.18 £

SA105

Other property income

Income

• Furnished holiday lettings profits	copy from box 5.14 5.19 £		
• Rents and other income from land and property	5.20 £	Tax taken off 5.21 £	
• Chargeable premiums	5.22 £		
• Reverse premiums	5.22A £		boxes 5.19 + 5.20 + 5.22 + 5.22A 5.23 £

Expenses (do not include figures you have already put in boxes 5.2 to 5.7 on Page L1)

• Rent, rates, insurance, ground rents etc.	5.24 £	
• Repairs, maintenance and renewals	5.25 £	
• Finance charges, including interest	5.26 £	
• Legal and professional costs	5.27 £	
• Costs of services provided, including wages	5.28 £	
• Other expenses	5.29 £	total of boxes 5.24 to 5.29 5.30 £
Net profit (put figures in brackets if a loss)		box 5.23 *minus* box 5.30 5.31 £

Tax adjustments

• Private use	5.32 £		
• Balancing charges	5.33 £		box 5.32 + box 5.33 5.34 £
• Rent a Room exempt amount	5.35 £		
• Capital allowances	5.36 £		
• Tick box 5.36A if box 5.36 includes a claim for 100% capital allowances for flats over shops	5.36A		
• Tick box 5.36B if box 5.36 includes enhanced capital allowances for environmentally friendly expenditure	5.36B		
• Landlord's energy saving allowance	5.36C £		
• 10% wear and tear	5.37 £		
• Furnished holiday lettings losses (from box 5.18)	5.38 £		total of boxes 5.35 to box 5.38 5.39 £
Adjusted profit (if loss enter '0' in box 5.40 and put the loss in box 5.41)			boxes 5.31 + 5.34 *minus* box 5.39 5.40 £
Adjusted loss (if you have entered '0' in box 5.40)		boxes 5.31 + 5.34 *minus* box 5.39 5.41 £	
• Loss brought forward from previous year			5.42 £
Profit for the year			box 5.40 *minus* box 5.42 5.43 £

Losses etc

• Loss offset against total income (read the note on page LN8)	5.44 £
• Loss to carry forward to following year	5.45 £
• Tick box 5.46 if these Pages include details of property let jointly	5.46
• Tick box 5.47 if **all** property income ceased in the year to 5 April 2006 **and** you don't expect to receive such income again, in the year to 5 April 2007	5.47

Now fill in any other supplementary Pages that apply to you.
Otherwise, go back to page 2 of your Tax Return and finish filling it in.

chapter 6: COMPUTING CAPITAL GAINS TAX

chapter coverage

In this chapter we see how to compute chargeable gains arising on the disposal of non-business assets. Chargeable gains arising on the disposal of business assets are not examinable in Unit 19 and are not considered here. You will study the computation of gains on business assets if you study unit 18.

We will see how to set allowable losses and taper relief against chargeable gains and how to arrive at the net gains taxable in any particular tax year.

Finally we will see how to compute the capital gains tax payable in any particular tax year.

The topics that we shall cover are:

- When does a chargeable gain arise?
- Computing chargeable gains and allowable losses
- Computing taxable gains in a tax year
- Computing capital gains tax payable

KNOWLEDGE AND UNDERSTANDING AND PERFORMANCE CRITERIA COVERAGE

knowledge and understanding

- The issues of taxation liability (Elements 19.1, 19.2, 19.3, 19.4)
- Basic law and practice (Elements 19.1, 19.2, 19.3, 19.4)
- Set-off capital losses, taper relief and annual exemption to arrive at taxable gains (Element 19.4)
- Calculation of capital gains tax payable on gains on non-business assets disposed of by individuals (Element 19.4)
- Calculation of gains and losses on disposals of non-business assets including indexation allowance (Element 19.4)

Performance criteria

- Identify and value disposed-of chargeable personal assets
- Calculate chargeable gains and allowable losses
- Apply reliefs and exemptions correctly
- Calculate capital gains tax payable
- Record relevant details of gains and capital gains tax payable legibly and accurately in the tax return

student notes

WHEN DOES A CHARGEABLE GAIN ARISE?

You saw in chapter one that, as a general rule, income is a receipt that is expected to recur (such as rental income), whereas a gain is a one off profit on the disposal of a capital asset (eg the profit on the sale of an investment property). For the gain on the disposal of a capital asset to be a chargeable gain there must be a CHARGEABLE DISPOSAL of a CHARGEABLE ASSET by a CHARGEABLE PERSON.

Chargeable persons

Individuals are the only type of chargeable person that you will meet in Unit 19.

Chargeable disposals

The following are the important chargeable disposals at Unit 19:

- Sales of assets or parts of assets
- Gifts of assets or parts of assets

A chargeable disposal occurs on the date of the contract (where there is one, whether written or oral), or the date of a conditional contract becoming unconditional.

The transfer of an asset on death is an EXEMPT DISPOSAL. On death the heirs inherit assets as if they bought them at death for their then market values. There is no capital gain or allowable loss on death.

Chargeable assets

All assets are chargeable assets unless they are specifically designated as exempt.

The following are the exempt assets that you need to be aware of:

- Motor vehicles suitable for private use
- Gilt-edged securities
- Qualifying corporate bonds (QCBs)
- Certain chattels (see later in this Course Companion)
- National Savings certificates and premium bonds
- Foreign currency for private use
- Investments held in an ISA
- Decorations for valour unless acquired by purchase.

student notes

Any gain arising on disposal of an exempt asset is not taxable and any loss is not allowable.

The exempt asset most commonly appearing in exam questions is a car. You should not waste time computing a gain or loss on a car. All you need to do is state that the car is an exempt asset, so no gain or loss arises.

Activity 1

Which of the following are chargeable assets for CGT purposes?

a) a diamond necklace

b) a cash sum invested in the National Lottery that ultimately results in a substantial win

c) a vintage Rolls Royce

COMPUTING CHARGEABLE GAINS AND ALLOWABLE LOSSES

Whenever a chargeable asset is disposed of, a calculation to determine the amount of any gain or loss is needed. The computation follows a standard format as shown below:

	£
Disposal consideration (or market value)	100,000
Less incidental costs of disposal	(1,000)
Net proceeds	99,000
Less allowable costs	(28,000)
Less enhancement expenditure	(1,000)
Unindexed gain	70,000
Less indexation allowance (if available)	(10,000)
Chargeable gain	60,000

We will now look at each of the items in the above pro-forma in turn.

Disposal consideration

Usually the disposal consideration is the proceeds of sale of the asset, but a disposal is deemed to take place at market value:

a) where the disposal is by way of a gift

b) where the disposal is made for a consideration which cannot be valued

c) where the disposal is made to a connected person (see below)

student notes

Costs

The following costs are deducted in the above proforma:

a) **Incidental costs of disposal**

These are the costs of selling an asset. They may include advertising costs, estate agents fees, legal costs or valuation fees. These costs should be deducted separately from any other allowable costs (because they do not qualify for any indexation allowance; see below, if it was available on that disposal).

b) **Allowable costs**

These include:

i) the original purchase price of the asset

ii) costs incurred in purchasing the asset (estate agents fees, legal fees etc).

Acquisition costs may qualify for an indexation allowance (from the month of acquisition) if it is available on the disposal.

c) **Enhancement expenditure**

ENHANCEMENT EXPENDITURE is capital expenditure which enhances the value of the asset and is reflected in the state or nature of the asset at the time of disposal.

Enhancement expenditure may qualify for an indexation allowance from the month in which it becomes due and payable.

Activity 2

Hal, a landlord, bought an investment property to let out for £500,000. He immediately spent £20,000 on an extension. However, by the time Hal sold the building the extension had been removed. Is the £20,000 deductible as enhancement expenditure?

The indexation allowance

Indexation was introduced to remove the inflationary element of a gain from taxation.

Individuals are entitled to an indexation allowance until April 1998, but not thereafter.

student notes

How it works

Molly bought a painting in June 1995 and sold it on 1 March 2006.

Indexation allowance is available for the period June 1995 to April 1998 only.

To calculate an indexation allowance, you need an indexation factor calculated from the month the asset was acquired to April 1998. You will be given this indexation factor in the examination. You will not be expected to calculate it. The indexation factor is multiplied by the cost of the asset to calculate the indexation allowance.

Similarly, indexation is available on enhancement expenditure. This expenditure is multiplied by an indexation factor that runs from the date the expenditure was incurred to April 1998.

How it works

An investment property was bought by an individual on 1 August 1984 for £200,000. Enhancement expenditure of £10,000 was incurred on 1 June 1996. The property was sold for £400,000 on 20 June 2005. Calculate the chargeable gain arising on the sale of the property. Assume indexation factors: August 1984 to April 1998 = 0.808; June 1996 to April 1998 = 0.063.

	£
Disposal proceeds	400,000
Less: purchase price	(200,000)
Less: enhancement expenditure	(10,000)
	190,000
Less: indexation on purchase price	
£200,000 × 0.808	(161,600)
indexation on enhancement expenditure	
£10,000 × 0.063	(630)
Chargeable gain	27,770

Activity 3

An individual bought a painting in July 1995 for £100,000. He sold the painting for £200,000 in August 2005. What is the chargeable gain on sale? Assume indexation factors July 1995 – August 2005 = 0.241 and July 1995 – April 1998 = 0.091

The indexation allowance cannot create or increase an allowable loss. If there is a gain before the indexation allowance, the allowance can reduce that gain to zero, but no further. If there is a loss before the indexation allowance, there is no indexation allowance.

student notes

Activity 4

Marak bought a painting for £50,000 in July 1995 and sold it for £40,000 in June 2005. What is the allowable loss? Assume an indexation factor July 1995 – April 1998 = 0.091

COMPUTING TAXABLE GAINS IN A TAX YEAR

An individual pays capital gains tax on any TAXABLE GAINS arising in a tax year.

Taxable gains are the net chargeable gains (gains minus losses) of the tax year reduced by unrelieved losses brought forward from previous years, a taper relief and the annual exemption. We will look at each of these items in turn.

Annual exemption

All individuals are entitled to the annual capital gains exemption. For 2005/06 it is £8,500. It is the last deduction to be made in computing taxable gains and effectively means that for 2005/06 the first £8,500 of taxable gains are tax free.

Activity 5

In 2005/06 Tina has the following gains and losses:

	£
Chargeable gains	27,000
Allowable losses	9,000

Tina had no allowable losses brought forward.

Compute Tina's taxable gains for 2005/06. Assume taper relief (see below) is not available.

Losses

Sometimes an allowable loss rather than a taxable gain arises. Once a loss has been calculated deal with it as follows:

a) firstly set it against gains arising in the same tax year until these are reduced to £Nil, then

b) set any remaining loss against net gains in the next tax year but only to reduce the net gains in the next year down to the amount of the annual exemption.

student notes

How it works

a) Tim has chargeable gains for 2005/06 of £25,000 and allowable losses of £19,000. As the losses are current year losses they must be fully relieved against the gains to produce net gains of £6,000, despite the fact that net gains are below the annual exemption.

b) Hattie has gains of £9,500 for 2005/06 and allowable losses brought forward of £6,000. Hattie restricts her loss relief to £1,000 so as to leave net gains of £(9,500 –1,000) = £8,500, which will be exactly covered by her annual exemption for 2005/06. The remaining £5,000 of losses will be carried forward to 2006/07.

c) Mildred has chargeable gains of £2,000 for 2005/06 and losses brought forward from 2004/05 of £12,000. She will leapfrog 2005/06 and carry forward all the brought forward losses to 2006/07. The gains of £2,000 are covered by the annual exemption for 2005/06.

Activity 6

Sally realised capital gains of £10,000 and allowable losses of £1,000 in 2005/06. She also had allowable losses of £3,000 brought forward from 2004/05. What amount of capital losses are carried forward to 2006/07?

Taper relief

After losses have been deducted from chargeable gains as described above, taper relief may be applied.

Taper relief reduces the percentage of the gain chargeable according to how many complete years the asset has been held since acquisition, or 6 April 1998, if earlier.

Taper relief is more generous for business assets than for non-business assets. In Unit 19 you will only be expected to compute gains on the disposal of non-business assets.

The percentages of gains that remain chargeable after taper relief are set out below.

student notes

Non-business assets No of complete years after 5 April 1998 for which asset held	*% of gain chargeable*
0	100
1	100
2	100
3	95
4	90
5	85
6	80
7	75
8	70
9	65
10 or more	60

The above percentages will be given in the tax tables at the beginning of the examination. Non-business assets acquired before 17 March 1998 qualify for an addition of 1 year (a bonus year) to the period for which they are actually held after 5 April 1998.

How it works

Pedro buys a painting on 1 June 2002 and sells it on 1 July 2005. For taper relief purposes Pedro held the asset for three complete years. This means that only 95% of the gain is chargeable after taper relief.

If the asset had been purchased in June 1996, only the complete years from April 1998 are counted. As this is a non-business asset acquired before 17 March 1998, this would give seven complete years of ownership plus an additional bonus year, so eight complete years in total. 70% of the gain is chargeable after taper relief.

Taper relief is applied to net chargeable gains after the deduction of current year and brought forward losses. The annual exemption is then deducted from the tapered gains. Remember that brought forward losses can only bring the gain before taper relief down to the amount of the annual exemption.

How it works

In 2005/06 Joanna made a gain of £25,000. She had losses brought forward from previous years of £5,000. The asset sold was a non-business asset that had been held for four complete years for taper relief purposes.

The brought forward losses are set against the gain to give net chargeable gains before taper relief of £20,000.

Taper relief is then applied to give a gain after taper relief of 90% x £20,000 = £18,000.

student notes

Finally the annual exemption is deducted to give a taxable gain of £9,500 (£18,000 – £8,500)

Activity 7

Toyah sold a non-business asset in May 2005 realising a chargeable gain of £40,000 before taper relief. She had purchased the asset in July 1997. Toyah made no other disposals in 2005/06 but she had allowable losses of £6,000 brought forward from 2004/05. What are Toyah's taxable gains after the annual exemption for 2005/06?

The allocation of losses

Allocate losses to gains in the way that produces the lowest tax charge. This means that you should deduct losses from the gains attracting the lowest rate of taper relief (ie where the highest percentage of the gain remains chargeable).

Example: allocation of losses to gains

Abdul made the following capital losses and gains in 2005/06:

	£
Loss	20,000
Gains (before taper relief)	
Asset A (non-business asset:	
90% of gain chargeable after taper relief)	30,000
Asset B (non-business asset:	
75% of gain chargeable after taper relief)	10,000

The best use of the loss is to offset it against the gain on asset A:

	£	£
Gain – Asset A	30,000	
Less loss	(20,000)	
Gain after taper relief (£10,000 × 90%)		9,000
Gain – Asset B	10,000	
Gain after taper relief (£10,000 × 75%)		7,500
Gains after taper relief		16,500
Less annual exemption		(8,500)
Taxable gains		8,000

Activity 8

In 2005/06 Ross sold a non-business asset that had been owned for 2 complete years realising a chargeable gain of £20,000. He also realised a gain of £50,000 on a non-business asset he had owned since 1994. At the start of 2005/06 he had bought forward losses of £10,000. Compute Ross' taxable gains for 2005/06.

COMPUTING CAPITAL GAINS TAX PAYABLE

student notes

We have seen above how to compute an individual's taxable gains for a tax year. In chapter 2 we saw that the rate of tax on taxable income depends on which income tax band income falls into. This also affects the rate of CGT as taxable gains are chargeable to capital gains tax as if the gains were an extra slice of income for the tax year concerned. CGT is due at 10% in the starting rate band, at 20% in the basic rate band and at 40% when total taxable income and taxable gains exceed £32,400.

The rate bands are used first to cover income and then gains.

How it works

Sally had taxable income in 2005/06 of £22,000. She made taxable gains (ie gains after deduction of the annual exemption) in the year of £20,000.

Sally's taxable income uses all the starting rate band of £2,090. However, £10,400 (£32,400 – £22,000) of the basic rate band remains to be used by the taxable gains. The remaining gain is taxed at 40%.

Capital gains tax payable

	£
£10,400 × 20%	2,080
£9,600 × 40%	3,840
£20,000	5,920

Activity 9

In 2005/06, Mustafa has the following income and net chargeable gains. Find the CGT payable.

	£
Employment income	30,000
Net chargeable gains	28,500

No taper relief is available.

CHAPTER OVERVIEW

- A chargeable gain arises when there is a chargeable disposal of a chargeable asset by a chargeable person
- Enhancement expenditure can be deducted in computing a chargeable gain if it is reflected in the state and nature of the asset at the time of disposal
- Individuals are entitled to an indexation allowance until April 1998. Indexation cannot create or increase a loss
- Taxable gains are net chargeable gains for a tax year minus losses brought forward minus the annual exemption
- Losses brought forward can only reduce net chargeable gains down to the amount of the annual exemption
- Taper relief reduces gains for individuals after 5 April 1998
- Losses should be allocated to the gains that attract the lowest taper relief (i.e. where the highest % of the gain remains chargeable)
- Taper relief is applied to an individual's net gains after the set off of current and brought forward capital losses
- The annual exemption is deducted after the application of taper relief
- CGT may be payable at 10%, 20%, or 40%
- The rate bands are applied first to taxable income and then to taxable gains

KEY WORDS

An individual is a **chargeable person**

A **chargeable asset** is any asset that is not an exempt asset

A **chargeable disposal** is a sale or gift of an asset.

An **exempt disposal** is a disposal on which no chargeable gain or allowable loss arises

Enhancement expenditure is capital expenditure that enhances the value of the asset and is reflected in the state or nature of the asset at the time of disposal

Taxable gains are the net chargeable gains of a tax year, after deducting losses, taper relief and the annual exemption

HOW MUCH HAVE YOU LEARNED?

1 Which of the following constitute chargeable disposals for CGT:

a) a gift of an antique necklace;
b) the sale of a building?

2 Yvette buys an investment property in April 2001 for £325,000. She sells the property on 12 December 2005 for £560,000. Show her gain on sale, after taper relief.

3 Sally bought a non-business asset in June 1990 for £30,000. She sold it for £50,000 in June 2005. No other disposals were made in 2005/06. Compute the gain arising after taper relief. Assume an indexation factor June 1990 to April 1998 = 0.283.

4 Philip has chargeable gains of £171,000 (no taper relief available) and allowable losses of £5,300 in 2005/06. Losses brought forward at 6 April 2005 amount to £10,000. What amount is liable to CGT in 2005/06? What are the losses carried forward?

5 Compute Martha's CGT liability for 2005/06, assuming she has:

Taxable income	£22,290
Chargeable gains (before AE)	£23,700

chapter 7: CHARGEABLE GAINS: ADDITIONAL ASPECTS

chapter coverage

In this chapter we look at how to compute chargeable gains when part of a chargeable asset is disposed of. We also see how to compute gains and losses arising on the disposal of chattels. Finally we look at the special rules that apply when disposals are made to connected people or between married couples.

The topics that we shall cover are:

- Part disposals
- Chattels
- Connected persons
- Married couples

KNOWLEDGE AND UNDERSTANDING AND PERFORMANCE CRITERIA COVERAGE

knowledge and understanding

- The issues of taxation liability (Elements 19.1, 19.2, 19.3, 19.4)
- Basic law and practice (Elements 19.1, 19.2, 19.3, 19.4)
- Identification of non-business assets disposed of including part disposals and personal shareholdings (Element 19.4)
- Calculation of gains and losses on disposals of non-business assets including indexation allowance (Element 19.4)

Performance criteria

- Identify and value disposed-of chargeable personal assets
- Calculate chargeable gains and allowable losses
- Apply reliefs and exemptions correctly

student notes

PART DISPOSALS

Sometimes part, rather than the whole, of an asset is disposed of. For instance, one third of a piece of land may be sold. In this case we need to be able to compute the chargeable gain or allowable loss arising on the part of the asset disposed of.

The problem is that although we know what the disposal proceeds are for the part of the asset disposed of, we do not usually know what proportion of the cost of the whole asset relates to that part. The solution to this is that we use the following fraction to determine the cost of the part disposed of.

The fraction is:

$$\frac{A}{A+B}=\frac{\text{value of the part disposed of}}{\text{value of the part disposed of + market value of the remainder}}$$

A is the proceeds (or market value) before deducting incidental costs of disposal.

You will need to learn the above formula for use in your exam.

The above formula is used to apportion the cost of the whole asset. If, however, any expenditure was incurred wholly in respect of the part disposed of, it should be treated as an allowable deduction in full for that part and not apportioned. An example of this is incidental selling expenses, which are wholly attributable to the part disposed of.

How it works

Mr Jones bought four acres of land for £270,000 in January 2001. He sold one acre of the land at auction in July 2005 for £200,000, before auction expenses of 15%. The market value of the three remaining acres is £460,000. Assume the land is a non-business asset. You are required to calculate Mr Jones' gain after taper relief.

Solution

The cost of the land being sold is:

$$\frac{200{,}000}{200{,}000+460{,}000}\times £270{,}000 = £81{,}818$$

student notes

	£
Disposal proceeds	200,000
Less: incidental costs of sale (15%)	(30,000)
Net proceeds	170,000
Less: cost (see above)	(81,818)
Gain before taper relief	88,182

Gain after taper relief (January 2001 – July 2005 = 4 years)

90% × £88,182 = £79,364

Activity 1

Yarrek bought a plot of land for investment purposes for £100,000 in May 1999. In January 2006, he sold part of the land for £391,000, which was net of legal fees on the sale of £9,000. At that time, the value of the remaining land was £600,000. Calculate the chargeable gain arising on the disposal in January 2006 after taper relief.

CHATTELS

A CHATTEL is tangible movable property (i.e. property that can be moved, seen and touched). Examples are items such as furniture and works of art.

A WASTING CHATTEL is a chattel with an estimated remaining useful life of 50 years or less. An example would be a racehorse or a greyhound. Wasting chattels are exempt from CGT (so that there are no chargeable gains and no allowable losses). There is one exception to this, but this is not assessable in Unit 19.

Activity 2

Jamiel bought a racing greyhound in June 2000 for £6,000. The greyhound was sold in August 2005 for £10,000. Calculate any chargeable gain arising.

There are special rules for calculating gains and losses on non-wasting chattels:

a) If a chattel is not a wasting asset, any gain arising on its disposal will still be exempt from CGT if the asset is sold for gross proceeds of £6,000 or less.

b) If sale proceeds exceed £6,000, the gain is limited to:

   5/3 × (gross proceeds – £6,000).

student notes

c) If sale proceeds are less than £6,000, any allowable loss is restricted to that which would arise if it were sold for gross proceeds of £6,000.

We will have a look at examples of each of these situations in turn.

How it works: gains on the disposal of non-wasting chattels

An individual art collector purchased a painting on 1 April 2002 for £3,000. On 1 January 2006 he sold the painting at auction.

Show the chargeable gain arising before taper relief if the sale proceeds were:

a) £3,600 net of the auctioneer's 10% commission
b) £7,200 net of the auctioneer's 10% commission

Solution

a) If the gross sale proceeds are £3,600 × 100/90 = £4,000 the gain arising on disposal of the chattel will be exempt

b) If the gross proceeds are £7,200 × 100/90 = £8,000 the gain arising on the disposal of the painting will be calculated as follows:

	£
Gross proceeds	8,000
Less: incidental costs of sale (10%)	(800)
Net proceeds	7,200
Less: cost	(3,000)
Gain before taper relief	4,200

Restricted to a maximum of 5/3 × £(8,000 – 6,000) = £3,333

Activity 3

On 1 May 2002 Jacky purchased a non-wasting chattel for £3,500. On 1 October 2005 she sold the chattel at auction for £9,500 (which was net of the auctioneer's 5% commission). Calculate the chargeable gain arising before taper relief.

How it works: losses

Magee purchased an antique desk on 1 July 2002 for £8,000. She sold the desk in July 2005 at auction for £4,750 net of auctioneer's fees of 5%.

Compute the gain or loss arising.

student notes

Solution

Magee obviously has a loss and therefore the allowable loss is calculated on deemed proceeds of £6,000. The costs of disposal can be deducted from the deemed proceeds of £6,000.

	£
Deemed disposal proceeds	6,000
Less: incidental costs of disposal (£4,750 × 5/95)	(250)
	5,750
Less: cost	(8,000)
Allowable loss	(2,250)

Activity 4

Jameel purchased a non-wasting chattel on 1 June 2003 for £8,800 which he sold in June 2005 at auction for £3,600 (which was net of 10% commission). Compute the allowable loss arising.

CONNECTED PERSONS

If a disposal is made to a connected person the disposal is deemed to take place at the market value of the asset.

If an allowable loss arises on the disposal, it can be set only against gains arising in the same or future years from disposals to the same connected person and the loss can only be set off if he or she is still connected with the person making the loss.

For this purpose an individual is connected with:

- his relatives (brothers, sisters, ancestors and lineal descendants)
- the relatives of his spouse
- the spouses of his and his spouse's relatives

Activity 5

On 1 August 2005 Holly sold a painting to her sister, Emily for £40,000. The market value of the painting on the date of sale was £50,000. Holly bought the painting on 1 September 2003 for £60,000.

What allowable loss arises on disposal of the painting and how may this be relieved?

student notes✍

MARRIED COUPLES

A husband and wife are taxed as two separate people. Each has an annual exemption, and losses of one spouse cannot be set against gains of the other.

Disposals between spouses do not give rise to chargeable gains or allowable losses. The disposal is said to be on a 'NO GAIN/NO LOSS' BASIS. The acquiring spouse takes the base cost of the disposing spouse, plus any indexation allowance to the date of the inter-spouse disposal, or 6 April 1998, if earlier.

The acquiring spouse normally takes over the taper relief position of the disposing spouse. This means the acquiring spouse is treated as acquiring the asset when the disposing spouse did.

CHAPTER OVERVIEW

- On the part disposal of an asset the formula A/A + B must be applied to work out the cost attributable to the part disposed of
- Wasting chattels are exempt assets for CGT purposes (eg racehorses and greyhounds)
- Non-wasting chattels are exempt if they are sold for gross proceeds of £6,000 or less. If gross proceeds exceed £6,000 any gain arising on the disposal of the asset is limited to 5/3 (Gross proceeds – £6,000)

KEY WORDS

A **no gain/no loss** disposal is a disposal on which no gain or loss arises.

A **chattel** is tangible movable property.

A **wasting chattel** is a chattel with an estimated remaining useful life of 50 years or less.

- If the gross proceeds are less than £6,000 on the sale of a non-wasting chattel, any loss otherwise arising is restricted by deeming the proceeds to be £6,000
- A disposal to a connected person takes place at market value
- For individuals, connected people are broadly brothers, sisters, ancestors, lineal descendants and their spouses plus similar relations of a spouse
- Losses on disposals to connected people can only be set against gains on disposals to the same connected person
- Disposals between spouses take place on a no gain/no loss basis

HOW MUCH HAVE YOU LEARNED?

1 Richard sells 4 acres of land in May 2005 out of a plot of 10 acres for £38,000. Costs of disposal amount to £3,000. The 10-acre plot cost £41,500 in 1987. The market value of the 6 acres remaining is £48,000.

Compute the chargeable gain/allowable loss arising before taper relief, assuming an indexation allowance of 0.620 to April 1998.

2 Mustafa bought a non-wasting chattel in 2004 for £3,500. Compute the gain arising before taper relief if he sells it in 2005 for

a) £5,800 after deducting selling expenses of £180
b) £8,200 after deducting selling expenses of £220

3 Simon bought a racehorse for £4,500 in May 2003. He sold the racehorse for £9,000 in June 2005. Calculate the gain arising before taper relief.

4 Santa bought a painting for £7,000 in June 2004. He sold the painting in June 2005 for £5,000. Calculate the allowable loss arising.

5 A loss arising on a disposal to a connected person can be set against any gains arising in the same year or in subsequent years. TRUE/FALSE?

6 No gain or loss arises on a disposal to a spouse. TRUE/FALSE?

chapter 8: SHARES

chapter coverage

In this chapter we will see how to compute chargeable gains and allowable losses on the disposal of shares. We assume that all shares disposed of are non-business assets as the disposal of business assets is not examinable in Unit 19.

This is a very important chapter as the computation of gains and losses on the disposal of shares is one of the examiner's favourite topics.

The topics that we shall cover are:

- Introduction
- Disposals by individuals
- The FA 1985 pool
- Bonus and rights issues

KNOWLEDGE AND UNDERSTANDING AND PERFORMANCE CRITERIA COVERAGE

<u>knowledge and understanding</u>

- The issues of taxation liability (Elements 19.1, 19.2, 19.3, 19.4)
- Basic law and practice (Elements 19.1, 19.2, 19.3, 19.4)
- Identification of non-business assets disposed of including part disposals and personal shareholdings (Element 19.4)

Performance criteria

- Identify shares disposed of by individuals

student notes

INTRODUCTION

Shares present special problems when computing gains or losses on disposal. For instance, suppose that a taxpayer buys some shares in X plc on the following dates:

	No of shares	*Cost*
		£
5 July 1990	100	150
17 January 1995	100	375
2 May 1998	100	1,000

On 15 June 2005, he sells 220 of his shares for £3,300. To determine his chargeable gain, we need to be able to work out which shares out of his three original holdings were actually sold. Since one share is identical to any other, it is not possible to work this out by reference to factual evidence.

As a result, it has been necessary to devise 'matching rules'. These allow the Revenue, on a disposal, to identify which shares have been sold and so work out what the allowable cost (and therefore the gain) on disposal should be. These matching rules are considered in detail below.

It is very important that you understand the matching rules. These rules are very regularly examined and if you do not understand them you will not be able to get any of this part of a question right.

Non-business assets

In Unit 19 it is only necessary to compute gains and losses arising on the disposal of non-business assets. Quoted shares in a trading company are non-business assets for taper relief purposes, provided:

a) the shareholder is not an officer or employee of the company; and

b) the shareholder does not own more than 5% of the voting rights in the company.

In addition, shares in a non-trading company are a non-business asset provided that the shareholder is not an officer or employee of the company or, broadly, that the shareholder does not have more than a 10% interest in the company.

DISPOSALS BY INDIVIDUALS

student notes

For individuals the matching of the shares sold is in the following order:

a) shares acquired on the same day;

b) shares acquired in the following thirty days on a FIFO (first in, first out) basis;

c) shares acquired between 6 April 1998 and disposal on a LIFO (last in, first out) basis;

d) shares from the Finance Act 1985 (FA 1985 pool) pool.

The composition of the FA 1985 pool is explained in detail below.

How it works

George bought the following shares in Red plc:

Date	*No of shares*	*Cost*
		£
1 May 2005	9,000	18,000
4 September 2005	2,000	5,000
12 March 2006	5,000	12,000

He sold 10,000 shares on 20 February 2006 for £30,000.

You are required to show George's gains on sale before taper relief.

Solution

Matching:

12 March 2006	5,000	shares (following 30 days)
4 September 2005	2,000	shares (LIFO)
1 May 2005	3,000	shares (LIFO)
	10,000	

student notes

Gains

	£	Gains £
12 March 2006 holding		
Proceeds 5/10 × £30,000	15,000	
Less: cost	(12,000)	
		3,000
4 September 2005 holding		
Proceeds 2/10 × £30,000	6,000	
Less: cost	(5,000)	
		1,000
1 May 2005 holding		
Proceeds 3/10 × £30,000	9,000	
Less: cost 3/9 × £18,000	(6,000)	
		3,000
Total gains		7,000

Activity 1

Selina bought shares in Green plc on the following dates:

	No.	£
1 June 2001	4,000	6,000
1 May 2004	1,000	2,000
1 August 2005	1,500	1,000

On 1 March 2006 she sold 3,000 shares for £8,000. Compute the gain or loss arising on the sale after taper relief.

THE FA 1985 POOL

The FA 1985 pool includes shares acquired between 6 April 1982 and 5 April 1998.

The calculation of the FA 1985 pool value

To compute the value of the FA 1985 pool, set-up three columns of figures:

a) the number of shares;
b) the cost of the shares ignoring indexation;
c) the indexed cost of the shares (ie cost plus indexation).

For historical reasons, your first step with a Finance Act 1985 pool should be to compute its value at 5 April 1985. To do this aggregate the indexed cost and number of shares acquired between 6 April 1982 and 5 April 1985 inclusive. In order to calculate the indexed cost of these shares, an indexation allowance, computed from the date of acquisition of the shares to April 1985, is added to the cost value.

student notes

How it works

Jackie bought 10,000 shares in X plc for £6,000 in August 1982 and another 10,000 for £9,000 in December 1984. Indexation factors are August 1982 – April 1985 0.157 December 1984 - April 1985 0.043

Compute the value of the FA 1985 pool at 6 April 1985.

	No of shares	*Cost*	*Indexed cost*
		£	£
August 1982 (a)	10,000	6,000	6,000
December 1984 (b)	10,000	9,000	9,000
	20,000	15,000	15,000
Index to April 1985			
£6,000 × 0.157 (a)			942
£9,000 × 0.043 (b)			387
Pool at 5 April 1985	20,000	15,000	16,329

Your second step should be to reflect all disposals and acquisitions of shares between 6 April 1985 and 5 April 1998 in the FA 1985 pool. Disposals/ acquisitions of shares that decrease/increase the amount of expenditure within the FA 1985 pool are called OPERATIVE EVENTS.

You must reflect each operative event in the FA 1985 pool. However, prior to reflecting an operative event within the FA 1985 share pool, a further indexation allowance (sometimes described as an indexed rise) must be computed up to the date of the operative event you are looking at. You must look at each operative event in chronological order.

How it works

Following on from the above example, now assume that Jackie acquired 4,000 more shares on 1 January 1990 at a cost of £6,000.

Show the value of the FA 1985 pool on 1 January 1990 following the acquisition. Assume an indexation factor April 1985 – January 1990 0.261

student notes

Solution

	No of shares	Cost £	Indexed cost £
6 April 1985	20,000	15,000	16,329
Index to January 1990			
£16,329 × 0.261			4,262
			20,591
January 1990 acquisition	4,000	6,000	6,000
	24,000	21,000	26,591

If there are several operative events, the procedure described must be performed several times over. In the case of a disposal, following the calculation of the indexed rise, the cost and the indexed cost attributable to the shares disposed of are deducted from the cost and the indexed cost within the FA 1985 pool. This is computed on a pro-rata basis if only part of the holding is being sold.

How it works

Continuing the above example, suppose that Jackie now disposes of 12,000 shares on 9 January 1995 for £26,000.

Show the value of the FA 1985 pool on 9 January 1995 following the disposal. Compute the gain on the disposal. Assume an indexation factor January 1990 – January 1995 0.222.

Solution

	No of shares	Cost £	Indexed cost £
Value at January 1990	24,000	21,000	26,591
Indexed rise to January 1995			
£26,591 × 0.222			5,903
	24,000	21,000	32,494
Disposal	(12,000)	(10,500)	(16,247)
Pool c/f	12,000	10,500	16,247

student notes

The gain on the disposal is calculated as follows:

	£
Sale proceeds	26,000
Less: cost	(10,500)
	15,500
Less: indexation (£16,247 – £10,500)	(5,747)
Gain	9,753

Note that the indexation is the difference for the shares sold between the indexed cost and the cost.

The above processes are repeated in the FA 1985 pool until it closes on 6 April 1998. This means that if a disposal takes place after 5 April 1998, your final step should be to close the FA 1985 pool on 6 April 1998 by calculating an indexation allowance up to April 1998. No further indexation is available on the shares after this date.

How it works

Continuing the above example, suppose that Jackie now disposes of 12,000 shares on 9 January 2006 for £40,000.

Compute the gain on the disposal. Assume indexation January 1995 to April 1998 = 0.114.

Solution

	No of shares	*Cost*	*Indexed cost*
		£	£
Value at January 1995	12,000	10,500	16,247
Indexed rise 1.95 – 4.98			
£16,247 × 0.114			1,852
Pool closes April 1998	12,000	10,500	18,099

Now that we have calculated the value of the FA 1985 pool at closure, we can calculate the chargeable gain or allowable loss arising on the disposal. The indexation allowance on the disposal is the difference between indexed cost of the shares being sold, and their cost. As usual, the indexation allowance cannot create or increase an allowable loss.

In this case the gain is computed as follows:

	£
Disposal proceeds	40,000
Less: cost	(10,500)
Unindexed gain	29,500
Less: indexation allowance £(18,099 – 10,500)	(7,599)
Gain before taper relief	21,901

student notes

Activity 2

Abduljabbar bought 4,000 shares in Green plc on 1 February 1986 for £5,000. He bought another 2,000 shares in Green Plc for £5,000 on 4 January 1995. There were no further acquisitions or disposals of these shares until 2,000 shares were sold in January 2006 for £9,000. Calculate the chargeable gain arising on the sale after taper relief. Assume indexation factors February 1986 – January 1995 = 0.511, January 1995 – April 1998 = 0.114

BONUS AND RIGHTS ISSUES

Bonus issues

BONUS SHARES are additional shares given free to shareholders based on their current holding(s).

Bonus shares are treated as being acquired at the date of the original acquisition of the underlying shares giving rise to the bonus issue. This means that shares deriving from a post April 1998 acquisition are treated as part of that holding whilst shares deriving from the FA 1985 pool are treated as though they are part of that pool.

Since bonus shares are issued at no cost there is no need to adjust the original costs. Instead the number of shares purchased at particular times are increased by the bonus issue. There is no need to index the 1985 pool to the date of the bonus issue. The normal matching rules apply.

How it works

Identify which of the following shares are sold:

1 April 1992	Purchase of 1,000 shares
1 May 2003	Purchase of 3,000 shares
1 May 2004	Bonus issue of 1 for 4
1 December 2005	Sale of 5,000 shares.

student notes

Solution

a) Order of matching:

i) 1 May 2003 purchase: then
ii) FA 1985 pool;

The bonus shares are related to the holding that gave rise to them. Let's see how this works below:

b) Numbers of shares matched with:

i)

	No. of shares
1.5.03	3,000
Bonus (1 for 4)	750
	3,750
Disposal 1.12.05	(3,750)

ii)

FA 1985 pool	No. of shares
1.4.92	1,000
Bonus (1 for 4)	250
	1,250
Disposal 1.12.05	(1,250)

Having identified the shares sold you can then calculate the chargeable gains/allowable losses arising. You can try this for yourself in the following activity.

Activity 3

Maria acquired shares in X Plc as follows:

	No.	£
19 August 1990	4,000	8,000
27 February 2001	6,000	15,000
5 March 2005	1 for 4 bonus issue	

On 1 May 2005 9,375 shares were sold for £20,000. Calculate the chargeable gains arising before taper relief. Assume an indexation factor August 1990 – April 1998 = 0.269

Rights issues

The difference between a bonus issue and a rights issue is that in a RIGHTS ISSUE the new shares are paid for. This results in an adjustment to the original cost.

Rights shares derived from shares in the 1985 pool go into that holding and those derived from post 5.4.98 holdings attach to those holdings. You should

student notes

add the number and cost of each of right issue to each holding as appropriate.

For the purposes of calculating the indexation allowance for rights issues before April 1998, expenditure on a rights issue is taken as being incurred on the date of the issue and not on the acquisition date of the original holding.

The length of the period of ownership for taper relief purposes depends on the date of acquisition of the original holding not the date of acquisition of the rights shares.

How it works

Richard acquired shares in A plc as follows:

1 June 1992	Bought 10,000 shares for £8,000.
1 October 2004	Took up rights issue of 1 for 5 at £1.00 per share.
1 August 2005	Bought 10,000 shares for £12,000.
1 April 2006	Sold 15,000 shares for £21,000.

Compute the gain arising on the disposal after taper relief. Richard made no other disposals in 2005/06. Assume an indexation factor: June 1992 – April 1998 = 0.167

Post 6 April 1998 acquisition (1 August 2005)

Applying the matching rules the 10,000 shares bought after 6 April 1998 are treated as disposed of first:

	£
Disposal proceeds $\left(\frac{10,000}{15,000} \times £21,000\right)$	14,000
Less: cost	(12,000)
Gain before taper relief	2,000

No taper relief is due.

Gain after taper relief = £2,000

student notes

Next deal with the FA 1985 pool. All the rights issue shares attach to that pool:

	No of shares	*Cost* £	*Indexed cost* £
FA 1985 Pool			
1.6.92	10,000	8,000	8,000
Index to April 1998			
£8,000 × 0.167			1,336
Pool closes	10,000	8,000	9,336
Rights issue	2,000	2,000	2,000
	12,000	10,000	11,336
Disposal	(5,000)	(4,167)	(4,723)
Pool c/fwd	7,000	5,833	6,613

	£
Disposal Proceeds $\left(\frac{5{,}000}{15{,}000} \times £21{,}000\right)$	7,000
Less: cost	(4,167)
Indexation (4,723 – 4,167)	(556)
Gain before taper relief	2,277

Taper relief is based on the length of ownership of the original shares (not the rights shares). This is 7 years post 6 April 1998 plus the additional year, so 8 years in total.

Gain after taper relief (70% × £2,277) = £1,594

Total gains after taper relief £1,594 + £2,000 = £3,594

Activity 4

Sarah acquired a shareholding in Y plc as follows:

1 August 1997	Bought 4,000 shares for £7,000
1 June 2003	Bought 2,000 shares for £6,000
1 June 2005	Took up rights issue 1 for 2 at £2.00 per share
1 December 2005	Sold 6,000 shares for £18,000

Compute the gain arising on the disposal, after taper relief (if applicable). Sarah made no other disposals in 2005/06. Assume an indexation factor August 1997 – April 1998 = 0.026.

CHAPTER OVERVIEW

- The matching rules for individuals are
  - Same day acquisitions
  - Next 30 days acquisitions on a FIFO basis
  - Acquisitions after 5.4.98 on a LIFO basis
  - Shares in the FA 1985 pool
- The FA 1985 pool runs from April 1982 to April 1998
- Bonus and rights shares are added to the shareholding to which they relate
- The difference between a bonus and a rights issue is that in a rights issue shares are paid for
- Indexation on rights issue shares runs from the date the rights were paid for. However, taper relief is based on the date the original shares were acquired

KEY WORDS

Operative events are disposals/acquisitions of shares that decrease/increase the amount of expenditure within the FA 1985 pool.

Bonus shares are shares that are issued free to shareholders based on original holdings.

Rights issues are similar to bonus issues except that in a rights issue shares must be paid for.

HOW MUCH HAVE YOU LEARNED?

1 State how 5,000 shares sold by an individual on 7 November 2005 would be matched with acquisitions, if the acquisitions were made as follows:

	No of shares
30 September 1987	2,000
10 July 1989	1,000
15 June 1999	3,000

2 What is an 'operative event' in the FA 1985 pool?

3 The amount paid to acquire further shares on a rights issue ranks for indexation from the date on which the original shares were acquired. TRUE/FALSE?

4 What is the difference between a bonus issue and a rights issue?

5 Sasha sold all her shares in T plc on 1 September 2005 for £24,000. She had bought the shares on the following dates.

	No of shares	*Cost*
		£
1 September 1985	2,000	1,700
1 March 2005	2,000	6,000

Calculate, before taper relief, the capital gains for 2005/06. Assume indexation factor September 1985 – April 1998 = 0.704

chapter 9: PRIVATE RESIDENCES

chapter coverage

In this chapter we look at the exemption that is available for any gain that arises on the disposal of an individual's private residence.

The topic that we shall cover is:

- Private residences

KNOWLEDGE AND UNDERSTANDING AND PERFORMANCE CRITERIA COVERAGE

knowledge and understanding

- The issues of taxation liability (Elements 19.1, 19.2, 19.3, 19.4)
- Basic law and practice (Elements 19.1, 19.2, 19.3, 19.4)
- Calculation of gains and losses on disposals of non-business assets including indexation allowance (Element 19.4)

Performance criteria

- Calculate chargeable gains and allowable losses
- Apply reliefs and exemptions correctly

student notes

PRIVATE RESIDENCES

A gain arising on the sale of an individual's only or main private residence (PRINCIPAL PRIVATE RESIDENCE) is exempt from CGT. Any loss is not allowable.

A husband and wife are entitled to only one principal private residence between them. This applies even though they are generally taxed independently.

The basic rule is that the gain is wholly exempt where the owner has occupied the whole of the residence throughout his period of ownership. Where occupation has been for only part of the period, the proportion of the gain exempted is:

$$\text{Total gain} \times \frac{\text{period of occupation}}{\text{total period of ownership}}$$

The last 36 months of ownership is exempt in all cases, if at some time the residence has been the taxpayer's main residence.

Activity 1

Clare bought herself a flat in April 2000 for £80,000. She lived in the flat until March 2003 when she moved to a farmhouse she had bought to be her main residence. The flat was empty until it was sold in March 2006 for £300,000. Calculate the chargeable gain, if any, arising on the disposal of the flat.

Deemed occupation

The period of occupation is also deemed to include certain periods of absence, provided the individual had no other main residence at that time and the period of absence was at some time both preceded by and followed by a period of actual occupation.

These periods of DEEMED OCCUPATION are:

a) any period (or periods taken together) of absence, for any reason, not exceeding three years. Where such a period exceeds three years, three years out of the longer period are deemed to be a period of occupation;

b) any periods during which the owner was required by his employment to live abroad;

c) any period (or periods taken together) not exceeding four years where the owner was:

student notes

1) self employed and forced to work away from home (UK and abroad); or

2) employed and required to work elsewhere in the UK (overseas employment is covered by (b) above).

A period of absence may be treated as deemed occupation under the above rules, even if the residence is let while the owner is away.

How it works

Mr A purchased a house for £50,000 on 31 March 1982. He lived in the house until June 1982. He was then sent to work abroad by his employer for ten years before returning to the UK to live in the house again in July 1992. He stayed in the house for six months before moving out to live with friends until the house was sold on 23 December 2005 for £150,000. You are required to calculate any chargeable gain arising on disposal. Assume indexation March 1982 to April 1998 = 1.047.

Solution

a) Exempt and chargeable periods

		Exempt months	*Chargeable months*
i)	April 1982 to June 1982	3	–
ii)	July 1982 to June 1992	120	–
iii)	July 1992 to December 1992	6	–
iv)	January 1993 to December 2002	–	120
v)	January 2003 to December 2005	36	–
		165	120

b) Explanations

i) *April 1982 to June 1982*. Actual occupation.

ii) *July 1982 to June 1992*. Covered by the exemption for periods of absence during which the owner is required by his employment to live abroad. The period is both preceded and followed by a period of owner occupation.

iii) *July 1992 to December 1992*. Actual occupation.

iv) *January 1993 to December 2002*. This period is not eligible to be partly covered by the exemption for three years of absence for any reason, as it is not followed by a period of actual occupation.

v) *January 2003 to December 2005*. Covered by the final 36 months exemption.

student notes

c) Calculation of the chargeable gain

	£
Disposal proceeds	150,000
Less: cost	(50,000)
Unindexed gain	100,000
Less: indexation allowance to April 1998:	
1.047 × £50,000	(52,350)
Indexed gain	47,650
Less: exempt under PPR provisions	
$\frac{165}{165+120} \times £47,650$	(27,587)
Gain before taper relief	20,063

Gain after taper relief (6 April 1998 to 5 April 2005 = 7 years plus additional year = 8 years)

70% × £20,063 = £14,044

In this example, had Mr A gone straight to live with friends in July 1992 instead of having six months occupation he would have lost not only the extra six months, but also the periods from July 1982 to June 1992, as these two periods of absence would lose their status of deemed occupation as the property was not occupied again by the owner prior to sale.

Activity 2

Shammima bought a house on 1 May 1999 for £80,000. She lived in the house until 30 April 2000 when she went to stay with her elderly mother for 2 years. Shammima returned to the house on 1 May 2002 and lived in it until 31 August 2002. She went to live in a new house she had bought on 1 September 2002. The first house was sold on 28 February 2006 for £200,000. Calculate the chargeable gain, if any, arising on disposal of the first house.

CHAPTER OVERVIEW

- Any gain arising on the disposal of an individual's principal private residence is exempt from CGT. A loss is not allowable
- Certain periods of non-occupation count as periods of deemed occupation
- The last 36 months of ownership always count as a period of occupation

KEY WORDS

A **principal private residence** is an individual's only or main residence

Periods of **deemed occupation** are periods during which an individual is treated as having occupied a residence

HOW MUCH HAVE YOU LEARNED?

1 Provided the property has at some time been the owner's principal private residence, the last .... months of ownership is always an exempt period. How many months?

2 Give three examples of periods of absence from a property which are deemed periods of occupation for the CGT principal private residence exemption.

3 Josephine purchased a house on 1 April 1990 for £60,000 and used it as her main residence until 10 August 1993 when she was sent by her employer to manage the Paris office. She worked and lived in Paris until 9 August 1997. Josephine returned to live in the house on 10 August 1997 but moved out to live in a new house (to be treated as her main residence) on 2 May 1999. The property was sold on 30 November 2005 for £180,000. Compute the gain on sale before tax relief. Assume indexation April 1990 to April 1998 = 0.300.

chapter 10: ADMINISTRATION AND PAYMENT OF INCOME TAX AND CGT

chapter coverage

In this chapter we look at when tax returns must be filed, for how long records must be kept and at the penalties chargeable for failure to comply with the requirements.

We then look at the due dates for payment of income tax and capital gains tax, and at the consequences of late payment.

Finally we consider the important topic of client confidentiality.

The topics that we shall cover are:

- Tax returns and keeping records
- Payment of tax, interest, surcharges and penalties
- Client confidentiality

KNOWLEDGE AND UNDERSTANDING AND PERFORMANCE CRITERIA COVERAGE

knowledge and understanding

- The duties and responsibilities of the tax practitioner (Elements 19.1, 19.2, 19.3, 19.4)
- The issues of taxation liability (Elements 19.1, 19.2, 19.3, 19.4)
- Basic law and practice (Elements 19.1, 19.2, 19.3, 19.4)
- Self assessment including payment of tax and filing of returns by individuals (Elements 19.1, 19.2, 19.3, 19.4)

Performance criteria

- Record income and payments accurately and legibly in the tax return
- Make computations and submissions in accordance with current tax law and take account of current Revenue Practice
- Maintain client confidentiality at all times
- Give timely and constructive advice on the maintenance of accounts and the recording of information relevant to tax returns
- Consult with Revenue staff in an open and constructive manner

student notes

TAX RETURNS AND KEEPING RECORDS

An individual's tax return comprises a Tax Form, together with supplementary pages for particular sources of income. You may have to complete the supplementary employment or the supplementary land and property pages in your exam. These forms were included for you to look at in earlier chapters in this Course Companion. You will be able to practice completing them when you try the practice exams later in the Course Companion.

Individuals who are chargeable to tax for any tax year and who have not received a notice to file a return are, in general, required to give notice of chargeability within six months from the end of the year ie by 5 October 2006 for 2005/06. The maximum penalty, where notice of chargeability is not given, is 100% of the tax assessed that is not paid on or before 31 January following the tax year.

Filing tax returns

The FILING DUE DATE for filing a return is the later of:

- 31 January following the end of the tax year that the return covers; eg for 2005/06 by 31 January 2007; and
- three months after the notice to file the return was issued.

If an individual wishes the Revenue to calculate his tax, earlier deadlines may apply. The filing date is normally the later of:

- 30 September following the tax year; eg for 2005/06, by 30 September 2006; and
- two months after notice to file the return was issued.

However, this earlier deadline does not apply to individuals issued with a four page short tax return. This form is used for taxpayers with simple tax affairs.

Penalties for late filing

The maximum penalties for filing a late tax return are:

a) Return up to 6 months late: £100
b) Return more than 6 months but not more than 12 months late: £200
c) Return more than 12 months late: £200 + 100% of the tax liability

In addition, a maximum penalty of £60 per day can be imposed where failure to deliver a tax return continues after notice has been given to the taxpayer. In this case the additional £100 penalty, imposed under b) if the return is more than six months late, is not charged.

The fixed penalties of £100/£200 can be set aside if the taxpayer had a reasonable excuse for not delivering the return. If the tax liability shown on the return is less than the fixed penalties, the fixed penalty is reduced to the amount of the tax liability. The tax geared penalty can also be reduced.

student notes

Keeping of records

Taxpayers must keep and retain all records required to enable them to make and deliver a correct tax return.

In general, records must be retained by tax payers until the later of:

a) i) 1 year after the 31 January following the tax year concerned

ii) 5 years after 31 January following the tax year concerned if the taxpayer lets property

b) provided notice to deliver a return is given before the date in a):

i) the time after which enquiries by the Revenue into the return can no longer be commenced

ii) the date any such enquiries have been completed.

Where a person receives a notice to deliver a tax return after the normal record keeping period has expired, he must keep all records in his possession at that time until no enquiries can be raised in respect of the return or until such enquiries have been completed.

The maximum penalty for each failure to keep and retain records is £3,000 per tax year.

Activity 1

The Revenue issued a tax return for 2005/06 to Myer on 3 September 2006. She filed this return on 31 March 2007. Myer calculates her own tax. State the date by which the return should have been filed and any penalties arising.

student notes

PAYMENT OF TAX, INTEREST SURCHARGES AND PENALTIES

Payments of tax

A taxpayer must make three payments of income tax:

Date	*Payment*
31 January in the tax year	1st PAYMENT ON ACCOUNT
31 July after the tax year	2nd payment on account
31 January after the tax year	Final payment to settle the remaining liability

Each payment on account is equal to 50% of the income tax payable (after the deduction of PAYE and tax suffered at source) for the previous year.

Capital gains tax must all be paid on 31 January following the tax year. There are no payments on account of capital gains tax.

How it works

Jeremy paid tax for 2005/06 as follows:

	£
Income tax payable	12,000
Capital gains tax payable	2,000

How much are the payments on account for 2006/07?

The income tax payable for 2005/06 was £12,000.

Each payment on account is £12,000/2 = £6,000

Payments are made on account of income tax but not on account of CGT.

Activity 2

Karen paid tax for 2005/06 as follows:

	£
Income tax payable	14,000
Capital gains tax	8,000

What payments on account must Karen make for 2006/07?

Payments on account are not required if the income tax payable for the previous year is less than £500.

Payments on account are normally fixed by reference to the previous year's tax liability but if a taxpayer expects his liability to be lower than this he may claim to reduce his payments on account to:

student notes

a) a stated amount, or
b) nil.

If the taxpayer's eventual liability is higher than he estimated he will have reduced the payments on account too far. Although the payments on account will not be adjusted, the taxpayer will suffer an interest charge on late payment.

The balance of any income tax, together with all CGT due for a year, is normally payable on or before the 31 January following the year.

How it works

Jameel made payments on account for 2005/06 of £7,500 each on 31 January 2006 and 31 July 2006, based on his 2004/05 liability. He later calculates his total income tax payable for 2005/06 at £20,000. In addition he calculated that his CGT liability for disposals in 2005/06 is £4,900.

What is the final payment due for 2005/06?

The final payment is the remaining income tax and all the CGT.

	£
Income tax (£20,000 – £7,500 – £7,500)	5,000
Capital gains tax	4,900
Final payment	9,900

In one case the due date for the final payment is later than 31 January following the end of the year. If a taxpayer has notified chargeability by 5 October but the notice to file a tax return is not issued before 31 October, then the due date for the payment is three months after the issue of the notice.

Surcharges

SURCHARGES are normally imposed in respect of balancing payments of income tax and any CGT

Paid	*Surcharge*
a) within 28 days of due date:	none
b) more than 28 days but not more than six months after the due date:	5%
c) more than six months after the due date:	10%

Surcharges apply to balancing payments of income tax and any CGT. The surcharges do not apply to late payments on account.

student notes

Interest

INTEREST is chargeable on late payment of both payments on account and balancing payments. In both cases interest runs from the due date until the day before the actual date of payment.

If a taxpayer claims to reduce his payments on account and there is still a final payment to be made, interest is normally charged on the payments on account as if each of those payments had been the lower of:

a) the reduced amount, plus 50% of the final income tax liability; and

b) the amount which would have been payable had no claim for reduction been made.

How it works

Harry made two payments on account of £2,500 each for 2005/06. The payments were made on 31 January 2006 and 31 July 2006. Harry had claimed to reduce these payments from the £4,000 that would have been due had they been based on his previous year's income tax liability.

Harry's 2005/06 tax return showed that his tax liabilities for 2005/06 (before deducting payments on account) were income tax: £10,000, capital gains tax: £3,000. Harry paid the balance of tax due of £8,000 on 30 September 2007.

For what periods and in respect of what amounts will Harry be charged interest?

The payments on account should have been £4,000 each. Interest will therefore be charged on the £1,500 not paid on 31 January 2006 until the date of payment 30 September 2007. Similarly interest will run on the other £1,500 that should have been paid on 31 July 2006 until 30 September 2007.

The final balancing payment should have been £13,000 – £8,000 = £5,000. Interest will run on £5,000 from the due date of 31 January 2007 until the date of payment 30 September 2007.

Repayment of tax and repayment supplement

Tax is repaid when claimed unless a greater payment of tax is due in the following 30 days, in which case it is set-off against that payment.

Interest is paid on overpayments of:

a) payments on account
b) final payments of income tax and CGT
c) penalties and surcharges

student notes

Interest runs from the original date of payment (even if this was prior to the due date), until the day before the date the repayment is made.

Enquiries

The Revenue can enquire into a return if they give written notice of this by

a) the first anniversary of the due filing date (not the actual filing date); or

b) if the return is filed after the due filing date, the quarter day following the first anniversary of the actual filing date. The quarter days are 31 January, 30 April, 31 July and 31 October.

A reason for raising an enquiry does not have to be given. In particular the taxpayer will not be advised whether he has been selected at random for an audit. Enquiries may be full enquiries, or may be limited to 'aspect' enquiries.

In the course of the enquiries the taxpayer may be required to produce documents, accounts or other information. The taxpayer can appeal against this.

The Revenue must issue a notice that enquiries are complete, and a statement of the amount of tax that should be included in the tax return, or the amount of a claim. The taxpayer then has thirty days to amend his return or claim to give effect to the conclusions. Alternatively, if the taxpayer is not satisfied he may, within 30 days, appeal.

Once an enquiry is complete, further enquiries cannot be made.

CLIENT CONFIDENTIALITY

Whenever you prepare accounts or returns on behalf of a client you should remember that you are bound by the ethical guideline of client confidentiality. This means that you should not discuss a client's affairs with third parties without the client's permission. You should also take care not to leave documents relating to a client's affairs in public places such as on trains or in restaurants.

CHAPTER OVERVIEW

- A tax return must be filed by the later of 31 January following a tax year and three months after the Revenue issue a notice requiring a return. Earlier dates may apply if the taxpayer requires the Revenue to calculate the tax
- Fixed penalties of £100/£200 apply if a return is filed up to/ more than six months late
- A tax geared penalty may apply if a return is filed more than 12 months late
- Individuals must keep records until the later of:

  a) i) 5 years after the 31 January following the tax year concerned if letting property; or

  ii) 1 year after the 31 January following the tax year concerned

  b) provided notice to deliver a return is given before the date in a):

  i) the time after which enquiries by the Revenue into the return can no longer be commenced; and

  ii) the date any such enquiries have been completed.
- Payments on account of income tax are required on 31 January in the tax year and on the 31 July following the tax year
- Balancing payments of income tax and all CGT is due on 31 January following the tax year
- Surcharges apply to balancing payments of income tax or any CGT. The surcharges do not apply to late payments on account
- Interest is chargeable on late payment of both payments on account and balancing payments
- The Revenue can enquire into a return if they give written notice of this by

  a) the first anniversary of the due filing date (not the actual filing date); or

  b) if the return is filed after the due filing date, the quarter day following the first anniversary of the actual filing date. The quarter days are 31 January, 30 April, 31 July and 31 October
- The ethical guideline of confidentiality means that you should never discuss a client's tax affairs with third parties without the client's permission

KEY WORDS

The **filing due date** is the date by which a return must be filed

Payment on account is an amount paid on account of income tax

Surcharges are normally imposed in respect of balancing payments of income tax and any CGT paid late

Interest is charged on late payments on account and on late balancing payments

HOW MUCH HAVE YOU LEARNED?

1 What are the due filing dates for income tax returns for 2005/06? Assume the taxpayer will calculate the tax due.

2 How will 2005/06 payments on account be calculated and when are they due?

3 A tax return for 2005/06 is issued in April 2006 and filed in May 2007. All income tax was paid in May 2006. No payments on account were due. What charges will be made on the taxpayer?

4 Sase filed her 2005/06 tax return on 28 January 2007. By what date must the Revenue give notice that they are going to enquire into the return?

5 Jamie, paid income tax of £12,000 for 2004/05. In 2005/06, his tax liability was £16,000.

State when payments must be made in respect of Jamie's 2005/06 income tax liability.

6 Tim should have made two payments on account of his 2005/06 income tax liability of £5,000 each. He actually made both of these payments on 31 August 2006.

State the amount of any surcharges due.

7 Zara has a CGT liability of £5,000 for 2005/06. State the date(s) by which this amount must be paid.

ANSWERS

ANSWERS TO CHAPTER ACTIVITIES

Chapter 1: Introduction

1

	Non-savings income	*Savings (excluding dividend) income*	*Dividend income*	*Total*
	£	£	£	£
Business income	44,000			
Building society interest		2,000		
Dividends			1,000	
	44,000	2,000	1,000	47,000
Less: personal allowance	(4,895)			
Taxable income	39,105	2,000	1,000	42,105

2 £160 × 100/80 = £200

3 Dividends £900 × 100/90 = £1,000
Interest £1,600 × 100/80 = £2,000

4

	£
Patent royalty £390 × 100/78	500
Copyright royalty	200
Charges on income	700

Chapter 2: Computing income tax payable

1

	Non-savings income	Savings *(excluding dividend) income*	*Total*
	£	£	£
Taxable income	25,000	35,000	60,000

	£
Tax on non-savings income	
£2,090 × 10%	209
£22,910 × 22%	5,040
£25,000	5,249
Tax on savings (excluding dividend) income	
£7,400 (£32,400 – £25,000) × 20%	1,480
£27,600 × 40%	11,040
£35,000	17,769

2

	Non-savings income	Savings (excluding dividend) income	Total
	£	£	£
	22,000	18,000	40,000

	£
Tax on non-savings income	
£2,090 × 10%	209
£19,910 × 22%	4,380
£22,000	4,589
Tax on savings (excluding dividend) income	
£10,400 (£32,400 – £22,000) × 20%	2,080
£7,000 (£5,460 × 100/78) × 20%	1,400
£600 × 40%	240
£18,000	8,309

Tutorial note. The basic rate band is extended by the gross amount of the personal pension premium paid.

3

	Non-savings income	Savings (excluding dividend) income	Dividend income	Total
	£	£	£	£
Rental income	20,000			
Bank interest (× 100/80)		10,000		
Dividends (× 100/90)			12,000	
	20,000	10,000	12,000	42,000
Less: personal allowance	(4,895)			
Taxable income	15,105	10,000	12,000	37,105

	£
Tax on non-savings income	
£2,090 × 10%	209
£13,015 × 22%	2,863
£15,105	
Tax on savings (excluding dividend) income	
£10,000 × 20%	2,000
Tax on dividend income	
£7,295 £(32,400 – 15,105 – 10,000) × 10%	729
£4,705 × 32.5%	1,529
	7,330
Less: tax credit on dividend	(1,200)
tax suffered on interest	(2,000)
Income tax payable	4,130

Chapter 3: Employment income

1

	£
Annual value	5,200
Additional benefit £(600,000 – 75,000) × 5%	26,250
	31,450
Less: rent paid	(12,000)
Taxable benefit	19,450

2

	£	£
Amount received 12,000 × 38p		4,560
Less: statutory limit		
10,000 × 40p	4,000	
2,000 × 25p	500	
		(4,500)
Taxable benefit		60

3 Round down CO_2 emissions to 195 g/km

Amount above baseline: 195 – 140 = 55 g/km

Divide by 5 = 11

Taxable % = 15% + 11% + 3% (diesel) = 29%

	£
Car benefit £30,000 × 29%	8,700
Fuel benefit £14,400 × 29%	4,176
Total benefit	12,876

Note. No deduction is made in respect of the amount paid towards the cost of private fuel.

4 *2004/05*

Benefit £6,000 × 20% = £1,200

2005/06

£6,000 × 20% × 3/12 = £300

Acquisition

	£	£
i) Market value at acquisition	4,000	–
ii) Market value when first provided	–	6,000
Less: assessed in respect of use £(1,200 + 300)	–	(1,500)
	4,000	4,500

Take higher, £4,500

5 $\frac{£6,200 + £5,200}{2} \times 5\% = £285$

As no elections are made, the 'average' method of valuing the loan is used.

Chapter 4: Employment income – additional aspects

1

	£
Ex-gratia payment	28,000
Company car (£8,800 × 6/12)	4,400
	32,400
Less: exemption	(30,000)
Taxable in 2005/06	2,400

2 Maximum contribution 15% × £105,600 (earnings cap) = £15,840

Chapter 5: Property income

1

	£	£
Rental income (£160 × 10)		1,600
		400
Less: bad debt	300	
interest	700	
		(1,000)
Net rental income		1,000

2

	£	£
Rental income: property 1		14,000
property 2 (3/12 × £6,800)		1,700
Less: agents fees (15% × £(14,000 + 1,700))	2,355	
insurance (3/12 × £1,200 + 9/12 × £1,400)	1,350	
(3/12 × £980 + 9/12 × £1,100)	1,070	
advertising for tenants	450	
		(5,225)
Net rental income		10,475

3

	£	£
Rental income		12,000
Less: water rates	800	
council tax	900	
agents fees	1,200	
wear and tear allowance		
10% × £(12,000 – 800 – 900)	1,030	
		(3,930)
Net rental income		8,070

Chapter 6: Computing capital gains tax

1 The diamond necklace only. The other assets are exempt assets.

2 As the £20,000 is not reflected in the state or nature of the building at the date of disposal, it is not deductible enhancement expenditure.

3

	£
Sale proceeds	200,000
Less: cost	(100,000)
	100,000
Less: indexation (£100,000 × 0.091)	(9,100)
Chargeable gains	90,900

Note. One of the indexation factors given in this activity was a 'red herring' (in other words a piece of information you didn't actually need was given to test if you know that you didn't need it). The examiner has said that she may give you indexation factors that are 'red herrings' in the examination.

4

	£
Proceeds	40,000
Less: cost	(50,000)
Allowable loss	(10,000)

Note. Indexation cannot increase an allowable loss.

5

	£
Gains	27,000
Less: losses	(9,000)
	18,000
Less: annual exemption	(8,500)
Taxable gains	9,500

6

	£
Capital gains	10,000
Less: allowable losses	(1,000)
	9,000
Less: capital losses	(500)
Chargeable gain b/f	8,500

Losses c/f £2,500 (£3,000 – 500)

7

	£
Gain	40,000
Losses b/f	(6,000)
Gain before taper relief	34,000

	£
Gain after taper relief 70% × £34,000	23,800
Less: annual exemption	(8,500)
Taxable gain	15,300

Note. The asset has been held eight years for taper relief purposes,. so 70% of the gain is taxable.

8

	£	£
Gain on non-business asset 1	20,000	
Less: loss b/f	(10,000)	
Gain after taper relief (not owned 3 years)		10,000
Gain on non-business asset 2	50,000	
Gain after taper relief 70% × £50,000		35,000
		45,000
Less: annual exemption		(8,500)
Taxable gain		36,500

9

	£
Employment income	30,000
Less: personal allowance	(4,895)
	25,105

Basic rate band remaining £32,400 – £25,105 = £7,295

Taxable gains £28,500 – £8,500 = £20,000

	£
CGT payable	
£7,295 × 20%	1,459
£12,705 × 40%	5,082
£20,000	6,541

Chapter 7: Chargeable gains: additional aspects

1

	£
Proceeds	391,000
Less: cost $\frac{400{,}000}{400{,}000+600{,}000} \times £100{,}000$	(40,000)
Gain before taper relief	351,000

Gain after taper relief (6 years) £351,000 × 80% = £280,800

2 No chargeable gain/allowable loss arises as greyhounds are exempt assets.

3

	£
Proceeds	10,000
Less: commission (5%)	(500)
	9,500
Less: cost	(3,500)
	6,000

Maximum gain 5/3 × £(10,000 – 6,000) = £6,667

Therefore, gain before taper relief = £6,000

4

	£
Deemed proceeds	6,000
Less: commission (£3,600 × 10/90)	(400)
	5,600
Less: cost	(8,800)
Allowable loss	3,200

5

	£
Deemed proceeds (market value)	50,000
Less: cost	(60,000)
Allowable loss	(10,000)

The loss may only be set against gains arising on the disposal of other assets from Holly to Emily.

Chapter 8: Shares

1 Match pool April 1998 disposals on a LIFO absis:

	£	Gains £
1 August 2005 (1,500 shares)		
Proceeds $\frac{1,500}{3,000}$ × £8,000	4,000	
Less: cost	(1,000)	
	3,000	
Gain after taper relief		3,000
1 May 2004 (1,000 shares)		
Proceeds $\frac{1,000}{3,000}$ × £8,000	2,667	
Less: cost	(2,000)	
	667	
Gain after taper relief		667
1 June 2001 (500 shares)		
Proceeds $\frac{500}{3,000}$ × £8,000	1,333	
Less: cost $\frac{500}{4,000}$ × £6,000	(750)	
	583	
Gain after taper relief (90% – 4 years)		525
Total gains after taper relief		4,192

2

	No of shares	*Cost* £	*Indexed cost* £
1 February 1986	4,000	5,000	5,000
Index to January 1995 0.511 × £5,000			2,555
			7,555
4 January 1995	2,000	5,000	5,000
	6,000	10,000	12,555
Index to April 1998 0.114 × £12,555			1,431
	6,000	10,000	13,986
6 April 1998 – pool closes	(2,000)	(3,333)	(4,662)
C/f	4,000	6,667	9,324

	£
Sale proceeds	9,000
Less: cost	(3,333)
Unindexed gain	5,667
Less: indexation (£4,662 – £3,333)	(1,329)
Gain before taper relief	4,338

Gain after taper relief (8 years) 70% × £4,338 = £3,037

3 *27 February 2001*

Number of shares	6,000
Bonus issue	1,500
	7,500

	£
Sale proceeds $\left(\frac{7,500}{9,375} \times £20,000\right)$	16,000
Less: cost	(15,000)
Gain before taper relief	1,000

19 August 1990

Number of shares	4,000
Bonus issue	1,000
	5,000

	£
Sale proceeds $\left(\frac{1,875}{9,375} \times £20,000\right)$	4,000
Less: cost $\left(\frac{1,875}{5,000} \times £8,000\right)$	(3,000)
	1,000
Less: indexation £3,000 × 0.269	(807)
Gain before taper relief	193

4 *Match June 2003 shares*

	No of shares	*Cost*
		£
Bought	2,000	6,000
Rights issue (1 for 2)	1,000	2,000
	3,000	8,000

	£
Disposal proceeds $\left(\frac{3,000}{6,000} \times £18,000\right)$	9,000
Less: cost	(8,000)
Gain before taper relief	1,000

For taper relief purposes the shares have been held for two years.

This means no taper relief available on this non-business asset.

Gain after taper relief = £1,000

August 1997 shares (FA 1985 pool)

	No of shares	*Cost*	*Indexed cost*
		£	£
August 1997	4,000	7,000	7,000
Index to April 1998			
£7,000 × 0.026			182
Pool closes	4,000	7,000	7,182
Rights issue	2,000	4,000	4,000
	6,000	11,000	11,182
Disposal	(3,000)	(5,,500)	(5,591)
Pool c/fwd	3,000	5,500	5,591

	£
Disposal proceeds	9,000
Less: cost	(5,500)
Less: indexation (5,591 – 5,500)	(91)
Gain before taper relief	3,409

For taper relief purposes the shares have been owned eight years (seven years plus the additional year).

Gain after taper relief 70% × £3,409 = £2,386

The total gain after taper relief is £2,386 + £1,000 = £3,386.

Chapter 9: Private residences

1 The gain arising on the disposal of the flat is completely exempt.

Clare was in actual occupation from April 2000 to March 2003.

The last 36 months of ownership are exempt because Clare had previously lived in the flat as her only or main residence.

2

	Actual or deemed occupation months	*Non-occupation months*
1 May 1999 to 30 April 2000	12	
1 May 2000 to 30 April 2002	24	
1 May 2002 to 31 August 2002	4	
1 September 2002 to 28 February 2003		6
1 March 2003 to 28 February 2006	36	
	76	6

	£
Sale proceeds	200,000
Less: cost	(80,000)
	120,000
Less: £120,000 × 76/82	(111,220)
Chargeable gain	8,780

Chapter 10: Administration and payment of income tax and CGT

1 Filing due date later of:

a) 31 January 2007
b) 2 December 2006

ie 31 January 2007.

A fixed penalty of £100 will be charged for the late filing, within six months of the due date.

2 Payments on account $\frac{£14,000}{2} = £7,000$

No payments on account are due in respect of CGT.

HOW MUCH HAVE YOU LEARNED? – ANSWERS

Chapter 1: Introduction

1 Building society interest (× 100/80) = £300

Interest received on individual savings account = £NIL (EXEMPT)

Dividends (× 100/90) = £160

2

	Non-savings income	*Dividend income*	*Total*
	£	£	£
Employment income	30,000		
Dividends (× 100/90)		300	
STI	30,000	300	30,300
Less: personal allowance	(4,895)		
Taxable income	25,105	300	25,405

3

	Non-savings income	*Savings (excluding dividend) income*	*Total*
	£	£	£
Rental income	3,000		
Building society interest (7,200 × 100/80)		9,000	
STI	3,000	9,000	12,000
Less: personal allowance	(3,000)	(1,895)	
Taxable income	NIL	7,105	7,105

The personal allowance is deducted first from non-savings income and then from savings (excl. dividend) income.

4

	Non-savings income	Savings (excluding dividend) income	Dividend income	Total
	£	£	£	£
Business profits	20,000			
Interest (× 100/80)		5,000		
Dividends (× 100/90)			4,000	
	20,000	5,000	4,000	29,000
Less: charges income (× 100/78)	(3,872)			
	16,128	5,000	4,000	25,128
Less: PA	(4,895)			
Taxable income	11,233	5,000	4,000	20,233

Chapter 2: Computing income tax payable

1 10%, 22% and 40%

2

	Non-savings income	Savings (excluding dividend) income	Dividend income	Total
	£	£	£	£
Employment income	4,000			
Interest (× 100/80)		16,000		
Dividends (× 100/90)			20,000	
	4,000	16,000	20,000	40,000
Less: personal allowance	(4,000)	(895)		
Taxable income	–	15,105	20,000	35,105

	£
Tax on savings (excluding dividend) income	
£2,090 × 10%	209
£13,015 × 20%	2,603
£15,105	
Tax on dividend income	
£17,295 × 10%	1,729
£2,705 × 32.5%	879
£20,000	
Income tax liability	5,420

3

	Non-savings income	Savings (excluding dividend) income	Dividends income	Total
	£	£	£	£
STI	10,000	2,000	3,000	15,000
Less: personal allowance	(4,895)	–	–	
Taxable income	5,105	2,000	3,000	10,105

	£
Tax on non-savings income	
£2,090 × 10%	209
£3,015 × 22%	663
£5,105	
Tax on savings (excluding dividend)	
£2,000 × 20%	400
Tax on dividend income	
£3,000 × 10%	300
Tax liability	1,572

The £2,000 of interest income clearly falls within the basic rate band so is taxed at 20%.

The £3,000 of dividend income also falls within the basic rate band so is taxed at 10%.

4 Basic rate tax relief is obtained by paying gift aid donations net of 22% tax. Additional relief is given by extending the basic rate band by the gross amount of the gift aid donation.

5

	Non-savings income	Savings (excluding dividend) income	Dividend income	Total
	£	£	£	£
Employment income	17,000			
Rental income	3,500			
Interest		3,800		
Dividends				
£6,500 × 100/90			7,222	
STI	20,500	3,800	7,222	31,522
Less: personal allowance	(4,895)			
Taxable income	15,605	3,800	7,222	26,627

	£
Tax on non-savings income	
£2,090 × 10%	209
£13,515 × 22%	2,973
Tax on savings (excluding dividend) income	
£3,800 × 20%	760
Tax on dividend income	
£7,222 × 10%	722
	4,664
Less: tax suffered at source	
tax credit on dividends	(722)
PAYE	(2,594)
tax suffered on interest	(760)
Tax payable	588

6

	Non-savings income £	*Savings (excluding dividend) income* £	*Dividend income* £	*Total* £
Business profits	29,000			
Building society interest (× 100/80)		5,000		
Dividends (× 100/90)			7,222	
	29,000	5,000	7,222	41,222
Less: personal allowance	(4,895)			
	24,105	5,000	7,222	36,327

	£
Tax on non-savings income	
£2,090 × 10%	209
£22,015 × 22%	4,843
Tax on savings (excluding dividend)	
£5,000 × 20%	1,000
Tax on dividend income	
£3,295 × 10%	329
£2,000 (extended) × 10%	200
£1,927 × 32.5%	626
	7,207
Less: tax credit on dividends	(722)
tax suffered on interest	(1,000)
Tax payable	5,485

Notes

1 In unit 19 you may, as here be required to include business profits in the income tax computation. However, you will not be required to compute business profits. The computation of business profits is assessed in unit 18 only.

2 The basic rate band is extended by the gross amount of the gift aid donation.

Chapter 3: Employment income

1 Self employed: contract for services

Employee: contract of service

2 Wholly, exclusively and necessarily.

3

	£
Amount received 8,000 × 35p	2,800
Less: 8,000 × 40p	(3,200)
Deductible amount	(400)

£400 is deductible in computing employment income.

4 £3,900, being the higher of the annual value and rent actually paid

5 FALSE. (Only those in occupation of 'job-related' accommodation can avoid a taxable benefit arising in respect of the accommodation.)

6 Not unless the employer is fully reimbursed, in which case the fuel benefit is NIL.

7 Benefit is based on the highest of:

		£	£
a)	current MV		325
b)	Original MV	500	
	Less: already assessed (in 2003/04)		
	£500 × 20%	(100)	400

ie £400

Therefore the taxable benefit after deduction of the amount paid (£150) is £250.

8 FALSE. Only if the loan does not exceed £5,000 is it ignored.

9 CO_2 emissions = 185 g/km (rounded down)

Above baseline 185 – 140 = 45 g/km

Divide by 5 = 45/5 = 9

Percentage = 15% + 9% = 24%

Benefit 24% × £24,000 = £5,760

10

	£
Car benefit (W)	21,600
Fuel benefit (£14,400 × 27%)	3,888
Telephone benefit	NIL
Total benefit	25,488

Working

Amount of emissions above baseline 200 – 140 = 60 g/km

Divide by 5 = 12

Percentage = 15% + 12% = 27%

£80,000 (maximum value) × 27% = £21,600

Chapter 4: Employment income – additional aspects

1 15%, taxable earnings

2 Individuals obtain basic rate tax relief by paying personal pension contributions net of 22% tax. Additional tax relief may be obtained by extending the basic rate band.

3 Form P45.

4 Form P11D is used by employers to report expense payments and benefits received by employees paid £8,500 + pa and directors. It must be submitted to the Revenue by 6 July following the tax year.

5 The first £30,000 of an ex-gratia redundancy payment is exempt from tax. Therefore:

	£
Payment	35,000
Less: exempt amount	(30,000)
Taxable amount	5,000

£5,000 is taxable in 2006/07 (the year it is received).

Chapter 5: Property income

1 Rental income 2005/06:

Rent accrued 1 December 2005 to 5 April 2006, ie 4/12 × £3,600 = £1,200.

2 Wear and tear allowance against rents:

10% × £(16,000 – 320 – 780) = £1,490

3 Insurance premiums accrued in 2005/06;

	£
6/12 × £4,800	2,400
6/12 × £5,200	2,600
	5,000

4 Rental losses are generally carried forward against future net rental profits. However if they arise from FHL they can be set against other income in the year of the loss and in the preceding year.

5 FHL income qualifies as net relevant earnings. Primarily this gives scope for relief for pension contributions.

6

	£
Rental income (£4,000 × 9/12)	3,000
Less: bad debt (£4,000 × 1/12)	(333)
expenses	(1,000)
Net rental income	1,667

Chapter 6: Computing capital gains tax

1 Both disposals are chargeable disposals.

2

	£
Proceeds	560,000
Less: cost	(325,000)
Gain before taper relief	235,000

Gain after taper relief (4 years) 90% × £235,000 = £211,500

3

	£
Sale proceeds	50,000
Less: cost	(30,000)
	20,000
Less: indexation (£30,000 × 0.283)	(8,490)
Gain before taper relief	11,510

Gain after taper relief (8 years, including bonus year) 70% × £11,510 = £8,057

4

	£
Gains	171,000
Less: current year losses	(5,300)
	165,700
Less: losses b/f	(10,000)
	155,700
Less: annual exemption	(8,500)
Taxable gain	147,200

There are no losses to carry forward.

5 Taxable income £22,290

	£
Basic rate band remaining (£32,400 – £22,290)	10,110
Taxable gain (£23,700 – £8,500)	15,200

		£
CGT	£10,110 × 20%	2,022
	£5,090 × 40%	2,036
	£15,200	4,058

Chapter 7: Chargeable gains: additional aspects

1

	£
Proceeds	38,000
Less: costs of disposal	(3,000)
Less: $£41,500 \times \frac{38,000}{38,000+48,000}$	(18,337)
	16,663
Less: indexation £18,337 × 0.620	(11,369)
Chargeable gain before taper relief	5,294

2 a) There is no gain or loss as the chattel is sold for gross proceeds of less than £6,000.

b)

	£
Net proceeds	8,200
Less: cost	(3,500)
	4,700

Gain cannot exceed 5/3 (8,420 – 6,000) = £4,033

Therefore, gain before taper relief is £4,033.

3 A racehorse is an exempt asset, so no chargeable gain or allowable loss arises.

4

	£
Deemed proceeds	6,000
Less; cost	(7,000)
Allowable loss	(1,000)

5 FALSE. A loss on a disposal to a connected person can be set only against gains arising on disposals to the same connected person.

6 TRUE.

Chapter 8: Shares

1 Match post April 1998 acquisitions on a LIFO basis:

	No.
15 June 1999	3,000
Disposal	(3,000)

Next match with FA 1985 pool which contains:

	£
30 September 1987	2,000
10 July 1989	1,000
Pool	3,000
Disposal	(2,000)
Pool shares remaining	1,000

2 An operative event is an acquisition or disposal of shares that needs to be reflected in the FA 1985 pool. It includes purchases, sales and rights issues. It does not include bonus issues.

3 FALSE. Rights issue shares rank for indexation only from the day on which they were acquired.

4 In a rights issue shares are paid for. In a bonus issue shares are not paid for.

5 First match with the March 2005 acquisition:

	£
Disposal proceeds	12,000
Less: cost	(6,000)
Gain before taper relief	6,000

Next match with the FA 1985 pool shares:

	No of shares	*Cost*	*Indexed cost*
		£	£
Purchase	2,000	1,700	1,700
Indexation 0.704 × £1,700			1,197
6 April 1998 pool closes	2,000	1,700	2,897

	£
Disposal proceeds	12,000
Less: cost	(1,700)
Less: indexation	(1,197)
Gain before taper relief	9,103

Chapter 9: Private residences

1 36

2 a) Any period (or periods taken together) of absence, for any reason, not exceeding three years. Where such a period exceeds three years, three years out of the longer period are deemed to be a period of occupation.

b) Any periods during which the owner was required by his employment to live abroad.

c) Any period (or periods taken together) not exceeding four years where the owner was:

1) self employed and forced to work away from home (UK and abroad)

2) employed and required to work elsewhere in the UK (overseas employment is covered by (b) above)

3

	£
Sale proceeds	180,000
Less: cost	(60,000)
	120,000
Less: indexation 0.300 × £60,000	(18,000)
Indexed gain	102,000

Principal private residence exemption

	Exempt months	*Chargable months*
1 April 1990 to 9 August 1993 (actual occupation)	40	
10 August 1993 to 9 August 1997 (employed abroad)	48	
10 August 1997 to 1 May 1999 (actual occupation)	21	
2 May 1999 to 30 November 2002		43
1 December 2002 to 30 November 2005 (last 36 months)	36	
	145	43

Exempt 145/188 × £102,000 = £78,670

Gain before taper relief £(102,000 – 78,670) = £23,330

Chapter 10: Administration and payment of income tax and CGT

1 The due date is the later of:

a) 31 January 2007
b) 3 months after a notice requiring the return was issued.

2 Payments on account of income tax for 2005/06 are due on:

31 January 2006; and
31 July 2006

Each payment on account due is equal to 50% of the prior year's income payable

3 £100 penalty (maximum) for failure to deliver return on time.

5% surcharge on tax paid late. Interest on tax paid late.

4 31 January 2008. A year after the due filing date

5

£6,000	31 January 2006
£6,000	31 July 2006
£4,000	31 January 2007

6 No surcharges are due on late payments on account.

7 31 January 2007.

REVISION COMPANION UNIT 19

chapter 1: INTRODUCTION

1 You act for Jonty. The following information is relevant for the year ended 5 April 2006:

1) His salary was £38,130.

2) His other income was:

	£
Building society interest	80
Dividends	63

Task

Compute Jonty's taxable income for 2005/06.

2 **Task**

Give brief details of the income tax implications of the following investments made by an adult individual in 2005/06 who has no other sources of income. Each investment is made by a different individual.

a) £3,000 invested in shares of ABC plc
b) £4,000 invested in an ISA.
c) £10,000 invested in a building society.

chapter 2: COMPUTING INCOME TAX PAYABLE

1 Mr Rich earned £55,000 from his employment in 2005/06. He paid tax of £9,700 under PAYE.

In 2005/06 he paid £11,700 (net) to Oxfam under the gift aid scheme.

Task

Calculate his tax payable.

2 Mr Poor took early retirement in 1996 when he was 55. He now works part-time. In 2005/06 his gross earnings were £4,000 and he paid tax under PAYE of £250. He received £900 in dividends, and £800 of building society interest. He received interest on his Midwest Savings Bank account totalling £80.

cHe pays £100 to a charity under the gift aid scheme.

Task

Calculate his tax payable/repayable.

chapter 3: EMPLOYMENT INCOME

1 a) James who earns £30,000 a year is given the use of a new television, costing £1,000, by his employer on 1 January 2004. James subsequently buys the television from his employer for £100 on 1 January 2006 when it is worth £300.

b) The television is used to keep James entertained when living at 3 Sims Court, London EC1, a flat provided by his employer for James. The flat cost £120,000, five years ago when James moved in, but due to a slump in property prices is now only worth £90,000. It has an annual value of £3,000. The official rate of interest is 5%.

Task

Calculate the value of James' taxable benefits in 2005/06.

2 Giles has worked for HiTech Computers Plc for many years and he has recently been promoted to sales manager, receiving a £5,000 pay rise from 1 July 2005. His revised salary is £35,000.

As a result of his promotion, he has been provided with a flat in London, due to being required to spend increasing amounts of time in London. The company pays £5,000 annual rent on the property, which has an annual value of £2,400. He is required to contribute £100 per month towards this.

Giles still has an interest free loan from the company for the purchase of his private car. The amount outstanding was £15,000 on 6 April 2005 and £10,000 on 5 April 2006. He has a car parking space provided in London under the Hi-Tech Computers Plc building, that costs the company £1,200 per annum.

Other perks that Giles receives are as follows:

1) Free medical insurance - the cost to the company is £385 per annum although if Giles had taken this out privately, he would have to pay £525 to cover both him and his wife.

2) £50 per week of child care vouchers to be used towards the provision of crèche facilities for his child who attends a private nursery.

3) A newspaper allowance of £20 per month.

Tasks

a) Calculate Giles' taxable salary for 2005/06.
b) Calculate the taxable benefits for 2005/06.

Assume that the official rate of interest is 5% for the whole of 2005/06.

3 Alf is employed by Red plc. Benefits for 2005/06 were as follows:

1) The company purchased hi-fi equipment for Alf's personal use at a cost of £800. The company retained ownership of the equipment.

2) Alf had exclusive use of a new 2.5 litre petrol engined car with a list price of £15,000. The emission rate is 185g/km. No petrol was provided for private motoring. The car is 2 years old.

3) Medical insurance was provided for £300.

4) Alf was given new suits of clothing which cost the company £400.

Task

Calculate Alf's taxable benefits for 2005/06.

4 Mr Bjork is chairman and chief executive of Peepop Ltd.

He receives a salary of £45,000 per annum and during the income tax year 2005/06 he is provided with the following benefits:

The company provided him with the use of a petrol engined Jaguar motor car costing £20,000 from 6 April 2005. The emission rate is 225g/km.

On 31 July 2005 he was involved in a serious road accident and the car was written off. He was charged with dangerous driving and the company met his legal costs of £2,000.

While he had use of the Jaguar, he contributed 50% of the cost of his private fuel.

When he resumed work on 1 October 2005, he was provided with a Mercedes car costing £30,000 and the use of a chauffeur. This car is used solely for business purposes. The emission rate is 195g/km.

Throughout the year, his wife, who is not employed by the company, has been provided with the use of a 2 litre BMW car costing £15,000 four years ago; the company meets all running costs and petrol bills. The emission rate is 245g/km.

He is provided with the use of video equipment which had been purchased by the company at a cost of £800 in total.

Task

Compute the total amount of benefits assessable on Mr Bjork for the income tax year 2005/06.

chapter 4: EMPLOYMENT INCOME – ADDITIONAL ASPECTS

1 Bill Wilson was employed as a works manager in a large company. He was made redundant on 1 January 2006. He received £35,000 compensation for loss of his job. This amount was not in return for services rendered to the company. His salary to 31 December 2005 was £33,597.

During his employment he was provided with a petrol engined BMW car which had a list price of £20,000. The CO_2 emissions of the car were 177 g/km. The company paid for all of the petrol.

Task

a) Calculate Bill's employment income for the tax year 2005/06.
b) Explain the PAYE procedures required in relation to Bill's termination of employment.

2 Kathy is employed as a sales representative and has an annual salary of £25,758. She contributes 5% of her gross salary to an occupational pension scheme.

Kathy uses her own car for all business journeys and claims the company's standard mileage allowance of 20.5p per mile. Total business miles travelled, and claimed for, amounted to 7,000 in 2005/06. Kathy always claims any expense entitlement against her earnings.

Kathy had an interest free loan from her employer obtained to help purchase a yacht. The average amount outstanding for the year 2005/06 amounted to £12,000.

In addition to the above Kathy also received in 2005/06:

	£
Building Society interest – amount credited to her account	300
Bank account interest – amount credited to her account	384

Task

Calculate Kathy's income tax payable for 2005/06.

Assume that the official rate of interest is 5% for the whole of 2005/06.

3 During 2005/06 Simon Harris had the following income:

	£
Salary	48,760
UK dividends (cash amount)	1,800
Building society interest (cash amount)	1,744

He works for a large UK company and was provided with the following benefits:

1) A diesel engined motor car with a list price of £10,667. The CO_2 emissions of the car are 155g/km. The company pays for all fuel used in the car.

2) An average outstanding loan of £8,000 to help purchase his main residence. The company charged him a flat rate of 2.75% interest. Simon had no other loans from any source.

3) Medical insurance. The company paid £575. A similar scheme would have cost Simon £650 if he had obtained the cover himself.

He paid £1,053 (gross) to a registered charity under the Gift Aid Scheme.

He also pays £6,000 (gross) to a personal pension plan.

Task

a) Calculate the income tax payable by Simon for the year 2005/06.

b) i) How will the company notify the Revenue of the benefits provided to Simon, and by what date must this be done?

   ii) How will the company notify the Revenue of the total pay paid to and the total tax deducted from Simon for the year? By what date must this be done?

Assume that the official rate of interest is 5% for the whole of 2005/06.

chapter 5: PROPERTY INCOME

1 Corelli owns three properties:

1) 5 Arnhem Avenue
2) 17 Blenheim Road
3) 27 Cannae Road.

All are let out unfurnished.

1) This was let until 5 July 2005 at an annual rental of £1,200. On 6 October 2005, it was let out to a new tenant on a 10-year lease agreement. The annual rental is £800.

2) This was let throughout 2005/06. The annual rental was £3,100. The rental due on 25 March 2006 was not received until 12 April 2006.

3) This was let from 6 July 2005 at an annual rental of £600.

Expenditure in connection with the properties was as follows:

		A	*B*	*C*
		£	£	£
Agent's commission	1 May 2005	25	35	10
	1 November 2005	25	35	10
Repairs (note)		–	100	1,800
Advertising for new tenants 10 July 2005		50	–	–

Note: The repairs in respect of property C are analysed as follows:

	£
Installation of new kitchen equipment	300
Retiling part of the roof after damage in May 2005	1,500

Task

Calculate the taxable rental income for 2005/06.

2 Jessica wishes to invest some money which she inherited, by buying accommodation in a popular UK holiday resort. She believes there are special conditions, which must be met for income derived from property to be treated as furnished holiday letting income.

Task

State the conditions that are necessary for a property to be treated as a furnished holiday letting.

chapter 6: COMPUTING CAPITAL GAINS TAX

1 Mattheus made gains of £16,900 (all on non-business assets owned for many years) and losses of £7,000 in 2005/06. He has losses brought forward of £5,000.

Task

Calculate the losses to carry forward to 2006/07.

2 Rita has taxable gains of £12,000 in 2005/06. She has taxable income of £26,000

Task

Calculate Rita's CGT payment for 2005/06.

3 John makes the following gains in 2005/06:

		£
Asset A	non-business, owned 4 years	5,000
Asset B	non-business owed 6 years	16,000

He makes a loss on Asset C of £2,500.

Task

Calculate taxable gains for 2005/06, after taper relief and annual exemption.

4 James acquired a chargeable asset in June 1992 at a cost of £6,000. In July 1992 the value of the asset was increased by enhancement expenditure of £2,000. The asset was sold in November 2005 for £40,300. The asset is not a business asset for taper relief purposes.

Task

Calculate the capital gains tax payable by James for 2005/06 assuming no other capital transactions and that he has taxable income of £26,300.

Use the following indexation factors:

June 1992 to April 1998 = 0.167
July 1992 to April 1998 = 0.171

5 Jim sold an investment property on 10 January 2006 for £180,000. It cost him £110,000 on 3 January 2001. The costs of purchase and sale were £220 and £2,350 respectively.

Task

Calculate the capital gain after taper relief.

chapter 7: CHARGEABLE GAINS: ADDITIONAL ASPECTS

1 Kidson purchased a plot of land on 1 January 1983 for £8,000. On 31 August 2005, he sold part of the land for £45,000 but declined an offer of £50,000 for the rest. The land is not a business asset for taper relief.

Task

Calculate the taxable gain arising on the sale assuming this is the only capital transaction Kidson has in 2005/06.

Use the following indexation factor:

January 1983 to April 1998 = 0.968

2 Peter sold his wife, Dora, a plot of land in August 2005 for £100,000. It was worth £150,000. Peter had acquired the land in July 2004 for £125,000.

Task

Explain Dora's base cost of the land.

3 Doug sold the following items on 1 August 2005:

1) A Ming vase bought in January 1984 for £2,000. The sales proceeds were £8,000.
2) A Leonardo cartoon bought in March 2000 for £7,200 and sold for £5,500.

Task

Calculate Doug's net chargeable gain for 2005/06 before the annual exemption and assuming he made no other disposals in the year.

Use the following indexation factor:

January 1984 to April 1998 = 0.872

chapter 8: SHARES

1 Mr Smith had the following transactions in shares in QRS plc. The shares are not businesses assets.

Date	No of shares bought/(sold)	Cost (proceeds)
	£	£
September 1982	2,000	3,000
November 1985	5,000	9,500
October 1987	(3,000)	(6,500)
May 2001	1,000	3,000
July 2005	(3,000)	(27,000)

His only source of income for 2005/06 was his salary of £30,000 from employment with the ABC partnership.

He made no other disposals of chargeable assets in 2005/06.

Task

Calculate the Capital Gains Tax liability of Mr Smith for 2005/06.

Use the following indexation factors:

September 1982 to April 1985 = 0.158
April 1985 to November 1985 = 0.012
November 1985 to October 1987 = 0.073
October 1987 to April 1998 = 0.580

2 Eloise's dealings in Moo plc were as follows:

	No of shares	Cost
		£
10 February 1986	12,000	18,000
10 April 2000	8,000	29,000
20 September 2000	Bonus issue of 1 for 4	Nil
15 March 2006	(12,000)	(48,000)

Task

Compute the chargeable capital gains assessable on the above disposal assuming the shares are not business assets for taper relief purposes.

Use the following indexation factor:

February 1986 to April 1998 = 0.683

3 Mark sold all his shares in AC plc on 4 November 2005 for £108,000. The shares had been acquired as follows:

	No of shares	Cost £
9 December 1986	12,000	4,400
12 October 1999 (rights issue 1:3 at £5)		
10 November 2005	2,000	11,500

The shares are not business assets for taper relief purposes.

Task

Calculate the chargeable gain arising.

Use the following indexation factor:

December 1986 to April 1998 = 0.632

chapter 9:
PRIVATE RESIDENCES

1 On 31 March 1982 Peter Stamp bought a private dwelling-house for £70,000, which he sold for £270,000 under a contract dated 3 July 2005.

He lived in this house as his only residence until 1 December 1995. From that date until the date of sale the property was unoccupied.

Task

Compute the chargeable gain before taper relief arising on the sale of the house.

Use the following indexation factor:

March 1982 to April 1998 = 1.047

chapter 10: ADMINISTRATION AND PAYMENT OF INCOME TAX AND CGT

1 You have received the following letter:

John Hunt
22 The Street
Anywhere
England

Peter Jones
'Tax Help for You'
16 The Road
London
England

16 September 2006

Dear Peter

Tax advice

I am employed as a general manager for Smith Brothers Ltd, based in Surrey. Up to now I have never had to complete a tax return before but recently I received a return from the Revenue, which I am not sure how to complete.

I have arranged, with your secretary, to meet with you on 2 October at 11.30 am.

I received and paid the following types of income and expenditure during the last tax year but I am not sure what information or documents you might require to complete the return.

Income

Salary (£32,000 approximately)
Loan of a company car
Private medical insurance provided by the company
Bank interest
Building Society interest
Interest from an Individual Savings Account

Payments

Contribution to a pension plan
Interest on a mortgage on my main residence
Subscription to the Institute of Personnel Managers

I would be grateful if you could inform me as to what I should bring with me to the meeting to help complete the tax return. Also could you answer the following questions?

a) When has the return to be returned to the Revenue?
b) When will the tax be paid and can I do it via my tax code?
c) Are there any penalties if the deadlines in (a) and (b) are not met, if so what are they?
d) My wife earns £6,500 a year – does this need to be included on my return?

Yours sincerely

John Hunt

Task

Reply to Mr Jones' letter.

PRACTICE EXAM 1
(SPECIMEN PAPER)

UNIT 19

Time allowed: 3 hours plus 15 minutes reading time

This exam is in TWO sections.

You must show competence in BOTH sections. You should therefore attempt and aim to complete EVERY task in EACH section.

You are advised to spend approximately 70 minutes on Section 1 and 110 minutes on Section 2.

All essential workings should be included within your answers, where appropriate.

SECTION 1 (Suggested time allowance: 70 minutes)

DATA

The date is May 2006. You work for Autumn Jewels Ltd in its payroll department. One of the employees, Phil Bright, has asked if you could help him complete his 2005/06 tax return.

From the company records, you determine that his taxable earnings comprise:

1 Annual salary of £18,500

2 Throughout the year, he was provided with a petrol-engined company car that had a list price of £28,600 when new. It has an emission rating of 177g/km. The company pays all running costs.

3 In July 2004 he was provided with a company loan of £20,000 on which he pays interest at 2.5% per annum. No capital repayment of the loan has been made.

4 He pays pension contributions to the employer's pension scheme at 5% of his salary.

Phil Bright gives you the following additional information:

1 He is 42 years old
2 He received dividend cheques of £5,400 during 2005/06
3 He also received building society interest of £4,160, net
4 He paid an annual subscription to his professional organisation of £250.

Task 1.1

Calculate the total assessable benefits for 2005/06.

Task 1.2

Prepare a schedule of income for 2005/06, clearly showing the distinction between non-savings, savings and dividend income. Phil Bright's personal allowances should be deducted, as appropriate.

Task 1.3

Calculate the net income tax payable for 2005/06, before deducting PAYE.

Task 1.4

Another employee, Beryl Simmons, has heard that you are helping Phil Bright sort out his tax. She asks you what you have been doing for Phil, so that she can see if you can also help her.

Discuss how you should reply to this request.

Task 1.5

Complete the attached tax return for employment income of Phil Bright.

Income for the year ended 5 April 2006

EMPLOYMENT

Name | **Tax reference**

Fill in these boxes first

If you want help, look up the box numbers in the Notes.

Details of employer

Employer's PAYE reference - may be shown under 'Revenue and Customs office number and reference' on your P60 or 'PAYE reference' on your P45

1.1

Employer's name

1.2

Date employment started (only if between 6 April 2005 and 5 April 2006)

1.3 / /

Date employment finished (only if between 6 April 2005 and 5 April 2006)

1.4 / /

Employer's address

1.5

Postcode

Tick box 1.6 if you were a director of the company

1.6

and, if so, tick box 1.7 if it was a close company

1.7

Income from employment

■ ***Money*** *- see Notes, page EN3.*

		Before tax
• Payments from P60 (or P45)		1.8 £
• Payments not on P60, etc.	- tips	1.9 £
	- other payments (excluding expenses entered below and lump sums and compensation payments or benefits entered overleaf)	1.10 £

	Tax taken off
• UK tax taken off payments in boxes 1.8 to 1.10	1.11 £

■ ***Benefits and expenses*** *- see Notes, pages EN3 to EN6. If any benefits connected with termination of employment were received, or enjoyed, after that termination and were from a former employer you need to complete Help Sheet IR204, available from the Orderline. Do not enter such benefits here.*

	Amount		Amount
• Assets transferred/ payments made for you	1.12 £	• Vans	1.18 £
• Vouchers, credit cards and tokens	1.13 £	• Interest-free and low-interest loans *see Note for box 1.19, page EN5.*	1.19 £
• Living accommodation	1.14 £	*box 1.20 is not used.*	
• Excess mileage allowance and passenger payments	1.15 £	• Private medical or dental insurance	1.21 £
• Company cars	1.16 £	• Other benefits	1.22 £
• Fuel for company cars	1.17 £	• Expenses payments received and balancing charges	1.23 £

SA101

BS 12/04net TAX RETURN ■ EMPLOYMENT: PAGE E1 *Please turn over*

Income from employment continued

■ ***Lump sums and compensation payments or benefits including such payments and benefits from a former employer***
Note that 'lump sums' here includes any contributions which your employer made to an unapproved retirement benefits scheme.

You must read page EN6 of the Notes ***before*** *filling in boxes 1.24 to 1.30.*

Reliefs

- £30,000 exception — 1.24 £
- Foreign service and disability — 1.25 £
- Retirement and death lump sums — 1.26 £

Taxable lump sums

- From box B of *Help Sheet IR204* — 1.27 £
- From box K of *Help Sheet IR204* — 1.28 £
- From box L of *Help Sheet IR204* — 1.29 £
- Tax taken off payments in boxes 1.27 to 1.29 - *leave blank if this tax is included in the box 1.11 figure and tick box 1.30A.* — Tax taken off 1.30 £
- Tick this box if you have left box 1.30 blank because the tax is included in the box 1.11 figure — 1.30A

■ ***Foreign earnings not taxable in the UK in the year ended 5 April 2006*** *- see Notes, pages EN6 to EN7* — 1.31 £

■ ***Expenses you incurred in doing your job*** *- see Notes, pages EN7 to EN8.*

- Travel and subsistence costs — 1.32 £
- Fixed deductions for expenses — 1.33 £
- Professional fees and subscriptions — 1.34 £
- Other expenses and capital allowances — 1.35 £
- Tick box 1.36 if the figure in box 1.32 includes travel between your home and a permanent workplace — 1.36

■ ***Seafarers' Earnings Deduction*** *(enter the amount of the earnings that attract the deduction, not the tax)* — 1.37 £

■ ***Foreign tax for which tax credit relief not claimed*** — 1.38 £

Student Loans

■ ***Student Loans repaid by deduction by employer*** *- see Notes, page EN8* — 1.39 £

- Tick box 1.39A if your income is under Repayment of Teachers' Loans Scheme — 1.39A

1.40 ***Additional information***

Now fill in any other supplementary Pages that apply to you.
Otherwise, go back to page 2 in your Tax Return and finish filling it in.

SECTION 2 (Suggested time allowance: 110 minutes)

DATA

You work for a firm of Chartered Accountants in the tax department. One of your clients, Jeanette Alsop, has had three capital transactions during the year 2005/06.

1 **Shares**

In January 2006, Jeanette sold all her shares in Purple Ltd for £45,000. These shares do not qualify as business assets. Your records show that her transactions in the shares of Purple Ltd were as follows:

Date	*Transaction*	*No of Shares*	£
April 1986	Purchased	300	3,000
May 1990	Purchased	500	8,500
June 1992	Bonus issue	1 for 5	
April 1995	Purchased	1,000	16,000
March 2002	Sold	400	7,600

2 **Motor car**

In November 2005, Jeanette sold a twenty-year old car that she has owned since April 1995. She originally paid £600 for the car, but sold it for £8,500.

3 **Land**

Jeanette bought 10 acres of land as an investment in August 1996 for £80,000. In February 2006, she sold 4 acres of this land to property developer for £71,000. The remaining 6 acres were valued at £95,000 on the date of sale.

Jeanette Alsop also owns a variety of properties that she rents out. The total rent receivable from these properties totalled £4,800 for 2005/06, of which she had received £4,000 by 5th April 2006. Of the remaining £800, £500 was deemed irrecoverable. She also had losses on her properties of £1,600 brought forward from 2004/05.

Task 2.1

Calculate the taxable gain or loss, after any taper relief, made on the disposal of the shares in Purple Ltd, if applicable.

Task 2.2

Calculate the taxable gain or loss, after any taper relief, made on the disposal of the car, if applicable.

Task 2.3

Calculate the taxable gain or allowable loss, after taper relief, made on the disposal of the land, if applicable.

Task 2.4

Calculate the property income chargeable to tax for 2005/06.

Task 2.5

Assuming Jeanette Alsop has no other income, calculate her tax liabilities for 2005/06, assuming that she is only entitled to the basic personal allowance.

Task 2.6

Jeanette Alsop informs you that when she completed her 2004/05 income tax return:

- She failed to declare £800 received from a building society
- All her other income in that tax year was taxed at basic rate, and totalled £300 short of the 40% tax band.
- As the building society interest had already suffered tax at source, she thought that she did not need to declare it.

She has heard that this was not the right thing to do, and she has sought your advice.

Using the headed paper provided write a memo to Jeanette Alsop advising her of the best course of action to take with regard to her dealings with the Inland Revenue, and the penalties, surcharges and/or interest she may have to pay when her mis-declaration is notified. You do not need to calculate the tax implications of this mistake.

MEMO

To: Jeanette Alsop
From: Accounting Technician
Date: 1 June 2006
Ref: Late declaration of income

This page is for the continuation of the e-mail. You may not need all of it.

Taxation tables

Tax rates and bands

	%	£
Starting rate	10	first 2,090
Basic rate	22	next 30,310
Higher rate	40	over 32,400

Savings income is taxed at 10%, 20% and 40%.
Dividends are taxed at 10% and 32.5%.

Personal allowances: £4,895

Car fuel charage

Set figure £14,400

Car benefit

Baseline for CO_2 emissions = 140 g/km

Inland revenue official rate: 5%

Capital gains tax

Annual exemption = £8,500

Indexation factors: April 1986 to May 1990 = 0.224
May 1990 to June 1992 = 0.111
June 1992 to April 1995 = 0.070
May 1990 to April 1995 = 0.181
April 1995 to April 1998 = 0.091
August 1996 to April 1998 – 0.062

Tapering relief for non-business assets:

Number of years held after 5 April 1998	*% of gain*
2 or less	100
3	95
4	90
5	85
6	80
7	75
8	70

PRACTICE EXAM 2
(DECEMBER 2003 PAPER)

UNIT 19

Time allowed: 3 hours plus 15 minutes reading time

This exam is in TWO sections.

You must show competence in BOTH sections. You should therefore attempt and aim to complete EVERY task in EACH section.

You are advised to spend approximately 80 minutes on Section 1 and 100 minutes on Section 2.

All essential workings should be included within your answers, where appropriate.

SECTION 1 (Suggested time allowance: 80 minutes)

DATA

The date is 1 December 2006. You work as a trainee accountant in the tax department of a firm of Chartered Accountants.

One of your friends, Joanne, has asked you to help her sort out her tax return for 2005/06.

Joanne supplies you with the following information:

1 She has an annual salary of £40,000.

2 Throughout the year, she was provided with a 1,800cc diesel-engined company car that had a list price of £21,200 when new. It has an emission rating of 172g/km. The company pays all running costs. Joanne pays her company £75 per month as a contribution for the private use of the car.

3 In January 2005, she was provided with a company loan of £15,000 on which she pays interest at 2% per annum. No capital repayment of the loan has been made.

4 Joanne received £250 from her company as reimbursement of entertainment costs she had incurred.

5 Her employer provides a non-contributory pension scheme, with the employer paying 8% of her salary to the pension scheme.

6 She received other income of:

	£
Cheques for dividends	1,548
Interest credited to ISA	360

Task 1.1

Calculate the total taxable benefits for 2005/06.

Task 1.2

Prepare a computation of taxable income for 2005/06, clearly showing the distinction between the different types of income.

Task 1.3

Calculate the net income tax payable for 2005/06, before deducting PAYE.

Task 1.4

Joanne does not know when she needs to complete her tax return for 2005/06. Joanne has not been issued with the new short tax return form.

Briefly explain:

a) The key dates for completion of a tax return

b) The implications, if any, of submitting a return during

   i) December 2006
   ii) February 2007

Task 1.5

During June 2006, Joanne bought a flat with the prime intention of renting it out. She immediately decorated the flat and bought several items of furniture. The flat has been rented out to tenants since July 2006. Joanne does not know about the tax implications for this source of income.

Explain to Joanne how:

a) her letting income is assessed
b) expenditure is allowed
c) any losses are relieved.

[You should assume the tax rules are the same in 2006/07 as 2005/06]

Task 1.6

Complete the tax return on the following pages for Joanne's employment income.

Income for the year ended 5 April 2006

EMPLOYMENT

Fill in these boxes first

Name	Tax reference
Joanne Harper	

If you want help, look up the box numbers in the Notes.

Details of employer

Employer's PAYE reference - may be shown under 'Revenue and Customs office number and reference' on your P60 or 'PAYE reference' on your P45

1.1

Employer's name

1.2 Sunny Dials

Date employment started (only if between 6 April 2005 and 5 April 2006)

1.3 / /

Date employment finished (only if between 6 April 2005 and 5 April 2006)

1.4 / /

Employer's address

1.5

Postcode

Tick box 1.6 if you were a director of the company

1.6

and, if so, tick box 1.7 if it was a close company

1.7

Income from employment

■ ***Money*** *- see Notes, page EN3.*

		Before tax
• Payments from P60 (or P45)	1.8	£
• Payments not on P60, etc. - tips	1.9	£
- other payments (excluding expenses entered below and lump sums and compensation payments or benefits entered overleaf)	1.10	£

		Tax taken off
• UK tax taken off payments in boxes 1.8 to 1.10	1.11	£

■ ***Benefits and expenses*** *- see Notes, pages EN3 to EN6. If any benefits connected with termination of employment were received, or enjoyed, after that termination and were from a **former** employer you need to complete Help Sheet IR204, available from the Orderline. Do not enter such benefits here.*

		Amount			Amount
• Assets transferred/ payments made for you	1.12	£	• Vans	1.18	£
• Vouchers, credit cards and tokens	1.13	£	• Interest-free and low-interest loans *see Note for box 1.19, page EN5.*	1.19	£
• Living accommodation	1.14	£	*box 1.20 is not used.*		
• Excess mileage allowance and passenger payments	1.15	£	• Private medical or dental insurance	1.21	£
• Company cars	1.16	£	• Other benefits	1.22	£
• Fuel for company cars	1.17	£	• Expenses payments received and balancing charges	1.23	£

SA101

BS 12/04net

TAX RETURN ■ EMPLOYMENT: PAGE E1

Please turn over

Income from employment continued

■ ***Lump sums and compensation payments or benefits including such payments and benefits from a former employer***
Note that 'lump sums' here includes any contributions which your employer made to an unapproved retirement benefits scheme.

You must read page EN6 of the Notes ***before*** *filling in boxes 1.24 to 1.30.*

Reliefs

- £30,000 exception — 1.24 £
- Foreign service and disability — 1.25 £
- Retirement and death lump sums — 1.26 £

Taxable lump sums

- From box B of *Help Sheet IR204* — 1.27 £
- From box K of *Help Sheet IR204* — 1.28 £
- From box L of *Help Sheet IR204* — 1.29 £
- Tax taken off payments in boxes 1.27 to 1.29 *- leave blank if this tax is included in the box 1.11 figure and tick box 1.30A.* — Tax taken off 1.30 £
- Tick this box if you have left box 1.30 blank because the tax is included in the box 1.11 figure — 1.30A

■ ***Foreign earnings not taxable in the UK in the year ended 5 April 2006*** *- see Notes, pages EN6 to EN7* — 1.31 £

■ ***Expenses you incurred in doing your job*** *- see Notes, pages EN7 to EN8.*

- Travel and subsistence costs — 1.32 £
- Fixed deductions for expenses — 1.33 £
- Professional fees and subscriptions — 1.34 £
- Other expenses and capital allowances — 1.35 £
- Tick box 1.36 if the figure in box 1.32 includes travel between your home and a permanent workplace — 1.36

■ ***Seafarers' Earnings Deduction***
(enter the amount of the earnings that attract the deduction, not the tax) — 1.37 £

■ ***Foreign tax for which tax credit relief not claimed*** — 1.38 £

Student Loans

■ ***Student Loans repaid by deduction by employer*** *- see Notes, page EN8* — 1.39 £

- Tick box 1.39A if your income is under Repayment of Teachers' Loans Scheme — 1.39A

1.40 ***Additional information***

Now fill in any other supplementary Pages that apply to you.
Otherwise, go back to page 2 in your Tax Return and finish filling it in.

BS 12/04net

TAX RETURN ■ EMPLOYMENT: PAGE E2

SECTION 2 (Suggested time allowance: 100 minutes)

DATA

One of your firm's clients, George Green, has had the following capital transactions during the year 2005/06:

1 **Shares**

In March 2006, George sold 2,000 of his shares in Crimson Ltd for £61,560. These shares do not qualify as business assets. His transactions in the shares of Crimson Ltd were as follows:

Date	*Transaction*	*No of Shares*	£
July 1989	Purchased	1,000	15,500
August 1993	Purchased	1,500	21,800
April 1995	Rights Issue	1 for 5	£10 each
May 2001	Sold	800	17,000
June 2003	Purchased	500	9,800

2 **Table**

George had bought an antique table in December 1985 for £1,200. He sold the table in October 2005 for £5,900.

3 **Land**

George bought 20 acres of land as an investment in January 1990 for £50,000. In November 2005, he sold 16 acres of this land to a property developer for £101,000. The remaining 4 acres were valued at £25,000 on the date of sale.

George has capital losses brought forward from 2004/05 of £20,000.

George also received the following income for 2005/06:

	£
Dividends from Crimson Ltd	7,650
Bank interest	720

Task 2.1

Calculate the taxable gain or loss made on the disposal of the shares in Crimson Ltd. Show the balance of shares to be carried forward for future disposal.

Task 2.2

Calculate the taxable gain or loss made on the disposal of the antique table, if applicable.

Task 2.3

Calculate the taxable gain or loss made on the disposal of the land.

Task 2.4

Calculate the total of taxable gains for the year.

Task 2.5

Calculate George's total income tax and capital gains tax liability for 2005/06.

Task 2.6

You received the following e-mail from George Green:

From: Ggreen@boxmail.net
To: AATStudent@boxmail.net
Sent:: 30 November 2006 9:12
Subject: Concerned

I have an issue that I would like to raise. I have some friends who use the same firm of accountants that I do.

This means that some people within the firm have access to information that I would not like my friends to know about. I am concerned that my tax affairs will not stay private because of this.

Awaiting your response,

George Green

Reply to George Green's e-mail, giving your response to his concern.

From: AATStudent@boxmail.net
To: Ggreen@boxmail.net
Sent:: 3 December 2006 14:57
Subject: Concerned

This page is for the continuation of the e-mail. You may not need all of it.

Taxation tables

Tax rates and bands

	%	£
Starting rate	10	first 2,090
Basic rate	22	next 30,310
Higher rate	40	over 32,400

Savings income is taxed at 10%, 20% and 40%.
Dividends are taxed at 10% and 32.5%.

Personal allowances: £4,895

Car fuel charge

Set figure £14,400

Car benefit

Baseline for CO2 emissions = 140 g/km

Inland revenue official rate: 5%

Capital gains tax

Annual exemption = £8,500

Indexation factors: July 1989 to August 1993 = 0.223
August 1993 to April 1995 = 0.054
April 1995 to April 1998 = 0.091
December 1985 to April 1998 = 0.693
January 1990 to April 1998 = 0.361

Tapering relief for non-business assets:

Number of years held after 5 April 1998	*% of gain*
2 or less	100
3	95
4	90
5	85
6	80
7	75
8	70

PRACTICE EXAM 3
(JUNE 2004 PAPER)

UNIT 19

Time allowed: 3 hours plus 15 minutes reading time

This exam is in TWO sections.

You must show competence in BOTH sections. You should therefore attempt and aim to complete EVERY task in EACH section.

You are advised to spend approximately 90 minutes on Section 1 and 90 minutes on Section 2.

All essential workings should be included within your answers, where appropriate.

SECTION 1 (Suggested time allowance: 90 minutes)

DATA

You work in the tax department of a firm of Chartered Accountants.

Your client, Averil Green, has given you the following information relating to the tax year 2005/06. She is employed by Emerald Ltd.

1 Her annual salary is £27,000, from which PAYE of £4,250 had been deducted.

2 Averil has the use of an apartment, which has an annual value of £5,500 and which cost Emerald Ltd £90,000. She makes no contribution towards the use of the apartment. She pays all the running costs of the apartment, which amounted to £3,200 for 2005/06. She does not have to live there to perform her job.

3 On 1 October 2005, Emerald Ltd provided Averil with a digital camera for her private use. It cost £500.

4 She received cheques for dividends of £720.

5 She received building society interest of £368.

6 She bought a house on 1 June 2005 for £84,000. She then bought furniture for £3,000 and let the house furnished for £5,000 per annum from 1 July 2005. The rent was paid quarterly in arrears. She also paid insurance of £450 for the period 1 June 2005 to 5 April 2006. She claimed the 10% wear and tear allowance for the furniture.

Task 1.1

Calculate the rental income for 2005/06.

Task 1.2

Calculate the total employment income, including benefits, for 2005/06.

Task 1.3

Prepare a computation of taxable income for 2005/06, clearly showing the distinction between the different types of income.

Task 1.4

Calculate the net income tax payable for 2005/06, after PAYE.

Task 1.5

Averil tells you that Emerald Ltd is thinking of providing her with a company car. It may pay for either all the petrol, or the petrol that relates to the business mileage only. She does not know what the tax implications of these benefits would be.

Explain to Averil, how:

- the benefit on company cars is calculated
- the benefit for fuel provided by Emerald Ltd is calculated
- any contribution she makes to Emerald Ltd for these benefits affects the taxable amounts

DATA

You received the following e-mail from Averil Green.

From:	averil00@emerald.co.uk
To:	AATStudent@boxmail.net
Sent:	10 June 2006 12:57
Subject:	Help

I was wondering if you could give me some tax advice. My father has high rental income and he has received a notification from the Revenue that shows how much tax he needs to pay. He agreed with the Revenue that his tax liability for 2004/05 was £7,580. My father thinks that his tax liability for 2005/06 is going to be about £10,000.

The notification from the Revenue reads:

The amounts due for 2004/05 are:

First payment on account £3,400 due by 31 January 2005
Second payment on account £3,400 due by 31 July 2005
Balancing payment £780 due by 31 January 2006

The payments on account due for 2005/06 are:

First payment on account £3,790 due by 31 January 2006
Second payment on account £3,790 due by 31 July 2006

My father has paid the tax due on 31 January 2006, but we don't understand how the Revenue arrived at these figures. Please explain how the Revenue has worked out these payment amounts and dates.

Many thanks.

Averil

Task 1.6

Reply to Averil's e-mail, answering her queries.

From: AATStudent@boxmail.net
To: averil00@emerald.co.uk
Sent: 18 June 2006 16:02
Subject: Re: Help

SECTION 2 (Suggested time allowance: 90 minutes)

DATA

One of the firm's clients, Adam Harrison, was 63 on 4 April 2006. He had the following capital transactions during the year 2005/06.

1 He bought a house on 1 October 1985 for £65,000. He lived in the house until 31 January 1988. He then worked abroad for exactly two years before returning to the UK to live in the house again. He took early retirement on 1 April 1994, moving to Portugal to live until 1 April 2003. He moved back into the house until 30 November 2005, when he sold it for £187,500.

2 On 1 July 2005, Adam sold 2,500 of his shares in Central Ltd for £75,800. The shares are not business assets for the purposes of taper relief. He had acquired 6,000 shares in Central Ltd in January 2001 for £140,160. In August 2004, Adam took up a rights issue of 1 for 10 at £8 per share.

3 On 1 February 2006, Adam sold an antique table for £15,000. He had bought it in July 1984 for £7,000 and had spent £1,000 in August 2001 on refurbishing it.

During the tax year 2005/06, Adam received:

1 a company pension of £2,000 per month;
2 £250 interest on an ISA.

Task 2.1

Calculate the taxable gain or loss made on the disposal of the house, after any taper relief, if applicable.

Task 2.2

Calculate the taxable gain or loss made on the disposal of the shares, after any taper relief, if applicable.

Task 2.3

Calculate the taxable gain or loss made on the disposal of the table, after any taper relief, if applicable.

Task 2.4

Calculate the capital gains tax liability for 2005/06.

DATA

You received the following e-mail from Adam Harrison.

From: Adam2Harris@boxmail.net
To: AATStudent@boxmail.net
Sent: 3 June 2006 16:12
Subject: Losses

I know that you have calculated all the necessary figures for my 2005/06 tax transactions, but I forgot to tell you that I have £6,000 capital losses from 2004/05 to bring forward.

Sorry if this will spoil the work that you have already done!

Awaiting your response

Adam Harrison

Task 2.5

Reply to Adam's e-mail, explaining to him how the losses from 2004/05 will affect his tax liability for 2005/06.

From: AATStudent@boxmail.net
To: Adam2Harris@boxmail.net
Sent: 18 June 2006 15:32
Subject: Re: Losses

This page is for the continuation of the e-mail. You may not need all of it.

Taxation tables

Tax rates and bands

	%	£
Starting rate	10	first 2,090
Basic rate	22	next 30,310
Higher rate	40	over 32,400

Savings income is taxed at 10%, 20% and 40%.
Dividends are taxed at 10% and 32.5%.

Personal allowances: £4,895

Car benefit percentage

The base level is 140g/km.
The base figure for petrol is £14,400.

Inland revenue official rate: 5%

Capital gains tax

Annual exemption = £8,500

Indexation factors: July 1984 to April 1998 = 0.824
October 1985 to April 1998 = 0.701

Tapering relief for non-business assets:

Number of years held after 5 April 1998	*% of gain*
2 or less	100
3	95
4	90
5	85
6	80
7	75
8	70

PRACTICE EXAM 4 (DECEMBER 2004 PAPER)

UNIT 19

Time allowed: 3 hours plus 15 minutes reading time

PRACTICE EXAM

This exam is in TWO sections.

You must show competence in BOTH sections. You should therefore attempt and aim to complete EVERY task in EACH section.

You are advised to spend approximately 90 minutes on Section 1 and 90 minutes on Section 2.

All essential workings should be included within your answers, where appropriate.

SECTION 1 (Suggested time allowance: 90 minutes)

DATA

You work in the tax department of a firm of Chartered Accountants.

You need to complete the computations for one of the clients, Joshua Howie, in preparation for entry onto the tax return.

From his employer records, you know that Joshua's employment income is as follows:

1. He works as a marketing manager, and has an annual salary of £28,000.
2. He pays 6% per annum into the company pension scheme, the employer contribution 8%.
3. Throughout the year, he had use of a 2,000cc petrol-engine company car that had a list price of £18,000 when new. It has an emission rating of 157g/km. The company pays all the running costs, including the petrol. Joshua pays his company £100 per month as a contribution for the private usage of the car.
4. In December 2005, the company provided Joshua with a computer to use at home. It cost £1,200 when new.

Joshua Howie gives you the following additional information:

1. He receives cheques for dividends of £765.
2. Interest credited to an ISA was £250.
3. He paid £160 to his professional marketing body as the annual subscription.

Task 1.1

a) Calculate the total taxable benefits for 2005/06.

b) Calculate the net employment income.

Task 1.2

Prepare a computation of taxable income for 2005/06, clearly showing the distinction between the different types of income.

Task 1.3

Calculate the net income tax payable for 2005/06.

Task 1.4

Joshua Howie has expressed concern that his personal tax information may be seen outside of the Tax Department within the firm of Chartered Accountants. He feels that this would compromise his right to privacy in his personal affairs.

How should you respond to this concern?

DATA

You have received the following email from Joshua Howie.

From: JoshuaHowie3@boxmail.net
To: AATStudent@boxmail.net
Sent: 2 December 2006 11:26
Subject: Accommodation

I have just found out that I could be relocated by the company to another city for some time. The company has a flat that I could use during that time, which is fully furnished and the company pays for all the running costs.

I have heard that it is an expensive flat and the running costs are high. I am worried that this will seriously affect the amount of tax that I pay, which doesn't seem fair if I need to live there to do my job.

Can you please explain all of the taxation aspects of this accommodation as a taxable benefit?

Awaiting your response,Joshua Howie

Averil

Task 1.5

Reply to Joshua's e-mail, explaining to him the various taxation aspects that can apply to the provision of accommodation.

From: AATStudent@boxmail.net
To: JoshuaHowie3@boxmail.net
Sent: 3 December 2006 15:32
Subject: Accommodation

SECTION 2 (Suggested time allowance: 90 minutes)

DATA

One of the firm's clients, Sarah Cartney, had the following capital transactions during the year 2005/06.

1 In July 2005, she sold 3,000 shares in A Ltd for £15,000. She acquired the shares as follows:

Date	*No of Shares*	£
September 1984	1,000	2,000
December 1990	1,000	3,000
July 1995	1,000	4,500

2 In October 2005, she sold all of her shares in B LTD for £25,500. She acquired the shares as follows:

Date	*No of Shares*	£
January 2002	3,000	14,800
August 2004	Bonus issue, 1 for 5	

3 In January 2006, she sold 5,000 of her shares in C Ltd for £12,000. She acquired the shares as follows:

Date	No of Shares	£
January 2003	6,000	18,000
December 2003	Rights issue, 1 for 50	900

4 In March 2006, she sold a picture for £5,000. She acquired it in April 1989 for £1,300.

Sarah owns a bungalow that she rents out for £500 per calendar month, payable on the first day of each month. She pays an agency 10% of the gross rent to run the letting for her. She paid £1,250 in the rates and repairs during 2005/06. Sarah made an allowable loss of £860 on this rental in 2004/05.

She has no other income.

Task 2.1

Calculate the chargeable gain or loss made on the disposal of the shares in A Ltd, before any taper relief, if applicable.

Task 2.2

Calculate the chargeable gain or loss made on the disposal of the shares in B Ltd, before any taper relief, if applicable.

Task 2.3

Calculate the chargeable gain or loss made on the disposal of the shares in C Ltd, before any taper relief, if applicable.

Task 2.4

Calculate the chargeable gain or loss made on the disposal of the picture, before any taper relief, if applicable.

Task 2.5

Calculate the net taxable gain for the year.

Task 2.6

Calculate the net property income for 2005/06.

Task 2.7

Calculate for 2005/06:

a) the total income tax liability

b) the total capital gains tax liability

Task 2.8

Complete the extract from the 2005/06 tax return for the property income pages attached.

UPDATE JANUARY 2005

The question paper gave a figure of '£1,250 in rates and repairs', on page 274. On reflection this was misleading as the tax return has one box labelled rates (5.24), and one labelled repairs (5.25). Students were therefore allowed to put any amount in either or both boxes provided they added up to £1,250.

Chief Assessor, PTC

Income for the year ended 5 April 2006

LAND AND PROPERTY

Name | **Tax reference**

Fill in these boxes first

If you want help, look up the box numbers in the Notes.

Are you claiming Rent a Room relief for gross rents of £4,250 or less?
(Or £2,125 if the claim is shared?)
Read the Notes on page LN2 to find out
- whether you can claim Rent a Room relief; and
- how to claim relief for gross rents over £4,250

Yes ☐ — If 'Yes', tick box. If this is your only income from UK property, you have finished these Pages

Is your income from furnished holiday lettings?
If not applicable, please turn over and fill in Page L2 to give details of your property income

Yes ☐ — If 'Yes', tick box and fill in boxes 5.1 to 5.18 before completing Page L2

Furnished holiday lettings

- **Income from furnished holiday lettings** — 5.1 £

■ ***Expenses*** (furnished holiday lettings only)

- Rent, rates, insurance, ground rents etc. — 5.2 £
- Repairs, maintenance and renewals — 5.3 £
- Finance charges, including interest — 5.4 £
- Legal and professional costs — 5.5 £
- Costs of services provided, including wages — 5.6 £
- Other expenses — 5.7 £ — total of boxes 5.2 to 5.7: 5.8 £

Net profit (put figures in brackets if a loss) — box 5.1 *minus* box 5.8: 5.9 £

■ ***Tax adjustments***

- Private use — 5.10 £
- Balancing charges — 5.11 £ — box 5.10 + box 5.11: 5.12 £
- Capital allowances — 5.13 £
- Tick box 5.13A if box 5.13 includes enhanced capital allowances for environmentally friendly expenditure — 5.13A ☐

Profit for the year (copy to box 5.19). If loss, enter '0' in box 5.14 and put the loss in box 5.15 — boxes 5.9 + 5.12 *minus* box 5.13: 5.14 £

Loss for the year (if you have entered '0' in box 5.14) — boxes 5.9 + 5.12 *minus* box 5.13: 5.15 £

■ ***Losses***

- Loss offset against 2005-06 total income — 5.16 £
- Loss - relief to be calculated by reference to earlier years — see Notes, page LN4: 5.17 £
- Loss offset against other income from property (copy to box 5.38) — see Notes, page LN4: 5.18 £

SA105

Other property income

■ *Income*

• Furnished holiday lettings profits	copy from box 5.14 5.19 £		
• Rents and other income from land and property	5.20 £	Tax taken off 5.21 £	
• Chargeable premiums	5.22 £		
• Reverse premiums	5.22A £		boxes 5.19 + 5.20 + 5.22 + 5.22A 5.23 £

■ *Expenses* (do not include figures you have already put in boxes 5.2 to 5.7 on Page L1)

• Rent, rates, insurance, ground rents etc.	5.24 £	
• Repairs, maintenance and renewals	5.25 £	
• Finance charges, including interest	5.26 £	
• Legal and professional costs	5.27 £	
• Costs of services provided, including wages	5.28 £	
• Other expenses	5.29 £	total of boxes 5.24 to 5.29 5.30 £

Net profit (put figures in brackets if a loss) — box 5.23 *minus* box 5.30 — 5.31 £

■ *Tax adjustments*

• Private use	5.32 £	
• Balancing charges	5.33 £	box 5.32 + box 5.33 5.34 £
• Rent a Room exempt amount	5.35 £	
• Capital allowances	5.36 £	
• Tick box 5.36A if box 5.36 includes a claim for 100% capital allowances for flats over shops	5.36A	
• Tick box 5.36B if box 5.36 includes enhanced capital allowances for environmentally friendly expenditure	5.36B	
• Landlord's energy saving allowance	5.36C £	
• 10% wear and tear	5.37 £	
• Furnished holiday lettings losses (from box 5.18)	5.38 £	total of boxes 5.35 to box 5.38 5.39 £

Adjusted profit (if loss enter '0' in box 5.40 and put the loss in box 5.41)		boxes 5.31 + 5.34 *minus* box 5.39 5.40 £
Adjusted loss (if you have entered '0' in box 5.40)	boxes 5.31 + 5.34 *minus* box 5.39 5.41 £	
• Loss brought forward from previous year		5.42 £
Profit for the year		box 5.40 *minus* box 5.42 5.43 £

■ *Losses etc*

• Loss offset against total income (read the note on page LN8)	5.44 £
• Loss to carry forward to following year	5.45 £
• Tick box 5.46 if these Pages include details of property let jointly	5.46
• Tick box 5.47 if **all** property income ceased in the year to 5 April 2006 and you don't expect to receive such income again, in the year to 5 April 2007	5.47

Now fill in any other supplementary Pages that apply to you.
Otherwise, go back to page 2 of your Tax Return and finish filling it in.

BS 12/04net

TAX RETURN ■ LAND AND PROPERTY: PAGE L2

Taxation tables

Tax rates and bands

	%	£
Starting rate	10	first 2,090
Basic rate	22	next 30,310
Higher rate	40	over 32,400

Savings income is taxed at 10%, 20% and 40%.
Dividends are taxed at 10% and 32.5%.

Personal allowances: £4,895

Car benefit percentage

The base level is 140g/km.
The base figure for petrol is £14,400.

Inland revenue official rate: 5%

Capital gains tax

Annual exemption = £8,500

Indexation factors: September 1984 to April 1985 = 0.052
April 1985 to December 1990 = 0.371
December 1990 to July 1995 = 0.148
July 1995 to April 1998 = 0.091

Tapering relief for non-business assets:

Number of years held after 5 April 1998	*% of gain*
2 or less	100
3	95
4	90
5	85
6	80
7	75
8	70

PRACTICE EXAM 5

UNIT 19

Time allowed: 3 hours plus 15 minutes reading time

PRACTICE EXAM

This exam is in TWO sections.
You must show competence in BOTH sections. You should therefore attempt and aim to complete EVERY task in EACH section.

You are advised to spend approximately 90 minutes on Section 1 and 90 minutes on Section 2.

All essential workings should be included within your answers, where appropriate.

SECTION 1 (Suggested time allowance: 90 minutes)

DATA

You work in the tax department of a firm of Chartered Accountants.

Your client, Sally Welch, is employed by Southern Ltd. She has given you the following information about the tax year 2005/06.

1 She earns an annual salary of £28,000. PAYE of £4,874 has been deducted.

2 Southern Ltd provides her with a car for business and private use. The car had a list price of £15,000 and has an emission rating of 192g/km. It has a diesel engine. Sally reimburses the company in full for the fuel she uses on private motoring.

4 Southern Ltd reimbursed Sally the sum of £200 in relation to business travel expenses.

4 Southern Ltd provides Sally with a mobile phone (cost to company £150) and laptop computer (cost to company £1,500), both of which are available for private use.

5 Sally owns two rental properties and has the following income and expenditure for 2005/06:

	£
Rental income due (of which £23,100 actually received in year, £1,100 is not recoverable)	26,400
Repairs	500
Interest on loan to buy properties	5,000
Letting agent's fees	1,500

Sally claims the wear and tear allowance. She had losses in relation to the lettings of £1,300 brought forward from 2004/05.

6 Sally had the following investment income:

	£
Building society interest	600
Dividends	1,800

7 Sally paid £400 per month during the year into a personal pension scheme.

Task 1.1

Calculate the taxable rental income for 2005/06.

Task 1.2

Calculate the total taxable benefits for 2005/06. Give brief explanations for how you treat each item.

Task 1.3

Compute the taxable income for 2005/06, clearly showing the distinction between the different types of income.

Task 1.4

Complete the tax return on the following pages for Sally's rental income.

Income for the year ended 5 April 2006

LAND AND PROPERTY

Fill in these boxes first

Name	Tax reference

If you want help, look up the box numbers in the Notes.

Are you claiming Rent a Room relief for gross rents of £4,250 or less?
(Or £2,125 if the claim is shared?)
Read the Notes on page LN2 to find out
- whether you can claim Rent a Room relief; and
- how to claim relief for gross rents over £4,250

Yes ☐ — If 'Yes', tick box. If this is your only income from UK property, you have finished these Pages

Is your income from furnished holiday lettings?
If not applicable, please turn over and fill in Page L2 to give details of your property income

Yes ☐ — If 'Yes', tick box and fill in boxes 5.1 to 5.18 before completing Page L2

Furnished holiday lettings

• Income from furnished holiday lettings		5.1 £
■ ***Expenses*** (furnished holiday lettings only)		
• Rent, rates, insurance, ground rents etc.	5.2 £	
• Repairs, maintenance and renewals	5.3 £	
• Finance charges, including interest	5.4 £	
• Legal and professional costs	5.5 £	
• Costs of services provided, including wages	5.6 £	
• Other expenses	5.7 £	total of boxes 5.2 to 5.7 5.8 £
Net profit (put figures in brackets if a loss)		box 5.1 *minus* box 5.8 5.9 £
■ ***Tax adjustments***		
• Private use	5.10 £	
• Balancing charges	5.11 £	box 5.10 + box 5.11 5.12 £
• Capital allowances	5.13 £	
• Tick box 5.13A if box 5.13 includes enhanced capital allowances for environmentally friendly expenditure	5.13A ☐	
Profit for the year (copy to box 5.19). If loss, enter '0' in box 5.14 and put the loss in box 5.15		boxes 5.9 + 5.12 *minus* box 5.13 5.14 £
Loss for the year (if you have entered '0' in box 5.14)	boxes 5.9 + 5.12 *minus* box 5.13 5.15 £	
■ ***Losses***		
• Loss offset against 2005-06 total income	5.16 £	
• Loss - relief to be calculated by reference to earlier years	see Notes, page LN4 5.17 £	
• Loss offset against other income from property (copy to box 5.38)	see Notes, page LN4 5.18 £	

SA105

BS 12/04net — TAX RETURN ■ LAND AND PROPERTY: PAGE L1 — *Please turn over*

Other property income

Income

• Furnished holiday lettings profits	5.19 £ (copy from box 5.14)		
• Rents and other income from land and property	5.20 £	Tax taken off 5.21 £	
• Chargeable premiums	5.22 £		
• Reverse premiums	5.22A £		boxes 5.19 + 5.20 + 5.22 + 5.22A 5.23 £

Expenses (do not include figures you have already put in boxes 5.2 to 5.7 on Page L1)

• Rent, rates, insurance, ground rents etc.	5.24 £	
• Repairs, maintenance and renewals	5.25 £	
• Finance charges, including interest	5.26 £	
• Legal and professional costs	5.27 £	
• Costs of services provided, including wages	5.28 £	
• Other expenses	5.29 £	total of boxes 5.24 to 5.29 5.30 £
Net profit (put figures in brackets if a loss)		box 5.23 *minus* box 5.30 5.31 £

Tax adjustments

• Private use	5.32 £		
• Balancing charges	5.33 £		box 5.32 + box 5.33 5.34 £
• Rent a Room exempt amount	5.35 £		
• Capital allowances	5.36 £		
• Tick box 5.36A if box 5.36 includes a claim for 100% capital allowances for flats over shops	5.36A		
• Tick box 5.36B if box 5.36 includes enhanced capital allowances for environmentally friendly expenditure	5.36B		
• Landlord's energy saving allowance	5.36C £		
• 10% wear and tear	5.37 £		
• Furnished holiday lettings losses (from box 5.18)	5.38 £		total of boxes 5.35 to box 5.38 5.39 £
Adjusted profit (if loss enter '0' in box 5.40 and put the loss in box 5.41)			boxes 5.31 + 5.34 *minus* box 5.39 5.40 £
Adjusted loss (if you have entered '0' in box 5.40)		boxes 5.31 + 5.34 *minus* box 5.39 5.41 £	
• Loss brought forward from previous year			5.42 £
Profit for the year			box 5.40 *minus* box 5.42 5.43 £

Losses etc

• Loss offset against total income (read the note on page LN8)	5.44 £
• Loss to carry forward to following year	5.45 £
• Tick box 5.46 if these Pages include details of property let jointly	5.46
• Tick box 5.47 if **all** property income ceased in the year to 5 April 2006 **and** you don't expect to receive such income again, in the year to 5 April 2007	5.47

Now fill in any other supplementary Pages that apply to you.
Otherwise, go back to page 2 of your Tax Return and finish filling it in.

BS 12/04net

TAX RETURN ■ LAND AND PROPERTY: PAGE L2

Task 1.5

Calculate the net income tax payable, after PAYE and any tax credits.

DATA

Sally is confused about how her income tax for 2005/06 will be paid. She knows that she had to pay a total of £4,500 in income tax by self assessment for 2004/05 and that she has, at your instructions, already paid something towards her tax bill for 2005/06.

Task 1.6

Write brief notes about how Sally will pay the income tax for 2005/06. You should also mention the 2006/07 position. Assume you are writing in June 2006.

SECTION 2 (Suggested time allowance: 90 minutes)

DATA

A client of your firm, Roger Gibson, has given you the following details to enable you to prepare a calculation of his capital gains tax liability for 2005/06:

1 Sold 6,000 shares in Cranmore Ltd in May 2005 for £13,800. These shares are non-business assets for taper relief. Roger bought 10,000 shares in March 1994 at a cost of £5,000. There was a 1 for 5 bonus issue in August 2001.

2 Sold 2 acres of land for £30,000 in August 2005. This was part of a 10 acre piece of land which he had bought in September 2000 for £50,000. The remaining 8 acres was worth £70,000 in August 2005. The land is a non-business asset for taper relief.

3 Sold a vase for £5,000 in September 2005. The vase cost Roger £7,500 in August 2001. The vase is a non-business asset for taper relief.

Roger is employed and earned a salary of £30,000 in 2005/06. He has no other income.

Task 2.1

Calculate the taxable gain made on the disposal of the shares, before any taper relief. State the taper relief ownership period.

Task 2.2

Calculate the taxable gain made on the disposal of the land, before any taper relief. State the taper relief ownership period.

Task 2.3

Calculate the allowable loss made on the disposal of the vase.

Task 2.4

Calculate the net taxable gains for 2005/06, after taper relief.

Task 2.5

Calculate the capital gains tax liability for 2005/06.

DATA

Roger has told you that he intends to sell a house on 31 July 2006. He bought the house on 1 August 1986 and lived there for 10 years. He then bought another house. He expects that gain on the sale to be £200,000.

He has been told that all or some of the gain may be reduced by capital gains tax reliefs. He does not expect to make any other disposals in 2006/07.

Task 2.6

Write a brief letter to Roger, explaining what reliefs are available and how much of the gain will be chargeable to CGT after these reliefs. You should assume that the rules about CGT are exactly the same in 2006/07 as in 2005/06.

Taxation tables

Tax rates and bands

	%	£
Starting rate	10	first 2,090
Basic rate	22	next 30,310
Higher rate	40	over 32,400

Savings income is taxed at 10%, 20% and 40%.
Dividends are taxed at 10% and 32.5%.

Personal allowances: £4,895

Car benefit percentage

The base level is 140g/km.
The base figure for petrol is £14,400.

Inland revenue official rate: 5%

Capital gains tax

Annual exemption = £8,500

Indexation factors: March 1994 to April 1998 = 0.141

Tapering relief for non-business assets:

Number of years held after 5 April 1998	*% of gain*
2 or less	100
3	95
4	90
5	85
6	80
7	75
8	70

REVISION COMPANION UNIT 19

answers

answers to chapter 1: INTRODUCTION

1 **Jonty**
Income tax computation 2005/06

	Non-savings income	*Savings income*	*Dividend income*	*Total income*
	£	£	£	£
Earnings	38,130			
Building society interest £(80 × 10/80)		100		
Dividends £(63 × 10/90)			70	
	38,130	100	70	38,300
PA	(4,895)			
Taxable income	33,235	100	70	33,405

2 a) **ABC plc shares**

A UK quoted company will normally pay out at least one dividend in the year to its shareholders. The dividend received is treated, in the shareholders hands, as income received net of a 10% tax credit. As it is unlikely that a £3,000 investment would generate gross dividends in excess of the individual's personal allowance, there will be no tax to offset this credit against. If there is no liability on the dividends the tax credit is lost. It cannot be repaid.

b) **ISA Investment**

The investments in an ISA will be free from income tax.

c) **Building Society interest**

An investment of cash into a building society account will result in the receipt of interest by the investor. This interest is paid net of lower rate tax at 20%. Unlike the notional credit on a dividend, this tax credit can be repaid to the individual if it results in an over-payment of tax credit.

answers to chapter 2: COMPUTING INCOME TAX PAYABLE

1 Mr Rich
Income tax computation 2005/06

		Non-savings income
		£
Earnings		55,000
PA		(4,895)
Taxable income		50,105
	£	£
Tax	2,090 @ 10%	209
	30,310 @ 22%	6,668
	15,000 @ 22% (W)	3,300
	47,400	
	2,705 @ 40%	1,082
Tax liability		11,259
Less: tax suffered at source (PAYE)		(9,700)
Tax payable		1,559

Working

Basic rate band extended by gross donation, ie (£11,700 × 100/78) + 32,400 = £47,400

2 Mr Poor
Income tax computation 2005/06

	Non-savings income	*Savings income*	*Dividend income*	*Total income*
	£	£	£	£
Earnings	4,000			
Dividends received (900 × 100/90)			1,000	
Building society interest (800 × 100/80)		1,000		
Bank deposit interest (80 × 100/80)		100		
STI	4,000	1,100	1,000	6,100
PA	(4,000)	(895)		
Taxable income	NIL	205	1,000	1,205

	£	£
Tax	205 @ 10%	20
	1,000 @ 10%	100
Tax liability		120
Less: tax credit on dividend		(100)
		20
Tax suffered at source		
Interest (£1,100 @ 20%)		(220)
PAYE		(250)
Tax repayable		(450)

Notes

1) The personal allowance is set off against non-savings income first, then against savings income.

2) The tax credit on the dividends can be deducted before other tax credits so as to maximise the repayment.

3) The charitable donation will extend the basic rate band, but as Mr Poor is not a higher rate taxpayer, the calculation is not necessary.

answers to chapter 3: EMPLOYMENT INCOME

1 a) During 2005/06 James will have a taxable benefit arising from the use of the asset:

	£
£1,000 × 20% × 9/12	150

He will also have a benefit when the asset is sold to him at an undervalue.

This will be the higher of the MV at the date of the 'gift' (less any contributions made by him).

	£
ie £(300 – 100)	200

and the original market value minus benefits assessed so far, again deducting his £100 contribution.

	£	£
Original market value		1,000
Assessed re use:		
2003/04 £1,000 × 20% × 3/12	50	
2004/05 £1,000 × 20%	200	
2005/06 £1,000 × 20% × 9/12	150	
		(400)
		600
Less: James' contribution		(100)
		500

Clearly £500 is the higher figure.

His total benefit in 2005/06 will therefore be £650.

b) The taxable benefit for use of the flat is calculated as follows:

	£
Annual value	3,000
£(120,000 – 75,000) × 5% (expensive accommodation)	2,250
	5,250

The original cost is used, not the value now.

2 a)

	£
Salary:	
April – June (3/12 × £30,000)	7,500
July – March (9/12 × £35,000)	26,250
Taxable salary	33,750

b)

	£
Accommodation	
Higher of i) Rent paid £5,000 × 9/12 = £3,750	3,750
ii) Rateable value 2,400 × 9/12 = £1,800	
Less: contribution (£100 × 9 months)	(900)
Loan interest $\frac{15{,}000+10{,}000}{2} \times 5\%$	625
Car parking space (not a benefit as near to place of work)	–
Medical insurance (cost to employer)	385
Crèche facilities (note 1)	–
Newspaper allowance	240
Taxable benefits 2005/06	4,100

Note. Child care vouchers of up to £50 a week are tax free.

3 **Benefits**

	£
Hi-fi equipment £(800 × 20%) (N1)	160
Car £(15,000 × 24%) (N2)	3,600
Medical insurance (N3)	300
Clothing (N3)	400
Taxable benefits 2005/06	4,460

Notes

1) The annual value of the hi-fi equipment is 20% of its cost.

2) The emission rate is 45g/km greater than 140g/km. The percentage is 15% + 45/5% = 24%.

3) The taxable value of the medical insurance and clothing is the cost to the company of providing the benefits.

4 **Mr Bjork's benefits**

	£
Jaguar: car (£20,000 × 32% × 4/12) (W1)	2,133
petrol (£14,400 × 32% 4/12) (W1)	1,536
Mercedes: no private use	
BMW: car (£15,000 × 35%) (W2)	5,250
petrol (£14,400 × 35%) (W2)	5,040
Legal costs	2,000
Use of video equipment £800 × 20%	160
Total taxable benefits	16,119

Workings

1) $\left(\frac{225-140}{5}\right) = 17 + 15 = 32\%$

2) $\left(\frac{245-140}{5}\right) = 21 + 15 = 36\%$ (35% Cap)

answers to chapter 4: EMPLOYMENT INCOME – ADDITIONAL ASPECTS

1 a)

	£
Salary	33,597
Redundancy £(35,000 – 30,000)	5,000
Car benefit (W2)	3,300
Fuel benefit (W3)	2,376
Employment income	44,273

Workings

1) *Taxable car %*

   CO_2 emissions above baseline

   175 g/km – 140 g/km = 35 g/km (round down)

   Divide by 5 = 35/5 = 7

   % = 15% + 7% = 22%

2) *Car benefit*

   22% (W1) × £20,000 × 9/12 = £3,300

3) *Fuel benefit*

   22% (W1) × £14,400 × 9/12 = £2,376

b) **PAYE procedures on termination of employment**

When an employee leaves employment, the employer must prepare a form P45 (Particulars of Employee Leaving).

The form shows details of the employee's income and tax paid to date.

The form is in four parts. One part is sent to the Revenue and three parts given to the employee.

One of the parts (part 1A) is the employee's personal copy.

If the employee takes up new employment, he hands the remaining two parts to his new employer.

2

	£	Non savings income £	Savings income £	Total income £
Salary	25,758			
Less: pension 5%	(1,288)			
	24,470			
Less: mileage allowance (W1)	(1,365)			
	23,105			
Benefit (W2)	600	23,705		
BSI £300 × 100/80			375	
Bank interest £384 × 100/80			480	
STI		23,705	855	24,560
Less: PA		(4,895)		(4,895)
Taxable income		18,810	855	19,665

	£		£
Tax	2,090 @ 10%		209
	(18,810 – 2,090) = £16,720 @ 22%		3,678
	855 @ 20%		171
Income tax			4,058
Less: tax on building society and bank interest			(171)
Income tax payable			3,887

Workings

1) *Statutory mileage rates*

	£
7,000 miles @ 40p	2,800
Less: allowed by company 7,000 @ 20.5p	(1,435)
Allowance	1,365

2 *Loan benefit*

£12,000 × 5% = £600

3 a)

	Non savings income	Savings income	Dividend income	Total income
	£	£	£	£
Salary	48,760			
Benefits:				
Car (W1)	2,240			
Fuel (W1)	3,024			
Loan (W2)	180			
Med. insurance	575			
UK dividends				
£1,800 × 100/90			2,000	
BSI £1,744 × 100/80		2,180		
STI	54,779	2,180	2,000	58,959
Less: personal allowance	(4,895)			(4,895)
Taxable income	49,884	2,180	2,000	54,064

		£
	£	
Tax	2,090 × 10%	209
	30,310 × 22%	6,668
	7,053 (W3) × 22%	1,552
	(49,884 – 32,400 – 7,053) = 10,431 × 40%	4,172
	2,180 × 40%	872
	2,000 × 32.5%	650
Tax liability		14,123
Less: dividend tax credit £2,000 × 10%		(200)
BSI tax deducted £2,180 × 20%		(436)
Tax payable		13,487

Workings

1) Taxable percentage 155 – 140 = 15 ÷ 5 = 3

   3% + 15% + 3% (diesel) = 21% Car = £10,667 × 21% = £2,240

   Fuel £14,400 × 21% = £3,024

2) Loan interest £8,000 × (5 – 2.75)% = £180

3) The basic rate band is extended by the gross Gift Aid donation ie £1,053 and the gross personal pension contribution £6,000 ie in total £7,053.

b) i) The company will notify the Revenue of the benefits provided to Simon by completing Form P11D.

   Form P11D must be submitted by 6 July 2006.

   ii) The company will notify the Revenue of the total pay paid to Simon and the tax deducted in the End of year return P14.

   Return P14 must be made by 19 May 2006.

answers to chapter 5: PROPERTY INCOME

1

	A	B	C
	£	£	£
Income			
(3/12 × £1,200 + 6/12 × £800)	700		
		3,100	
(9/12 × £600)			450
Expenditure			
Agent's commission: 1 May 2005	(25)	(35)	(10)
1 November 2005	(25)	(35)	(10)
Repairs	–	(100)	(1,500)
Advertising	(50)	–	–
	600	2,930	(1,070)

Net rent income = £2,460

Note. Installation of kitchen equipment is a capital expense so not deductible.

2 **Furnished holiday letting**

For a property to be assessed under the furnished holiday letting rules it must, broadly, be:

a) Furnished accommodation let on commercial basis with a view to realisation of profit

b) Situated in the UK

c) Available for commercial letting to the public for not less than 140 days in a tax year

d) Actually let for 70 days within the 140 day period

e) Not more than 155 days of the tax year must fall during periods of longer term occupation. Longer term occupation is described as a continuous period of more than 31 days during which the accommodation is in the same occupation.

answers to chapter 6: COMPUTING CAPITAL GAINS TAX

1

	£
Gains	16,900
Losses	(7,000)
	9,900
Losses b/f (9,900 – 8,500)	(1,400)
	8,500
Less: annual exemption	(8,500)
Taxable gains	NIL

Losses c/f (5,000 – 1,400) = £3,600

Taper relief is effectively lost as it applies after losses are deducted.

2

	£		£
Tax	6,400	@ 20% (W)	1,280
	5,600	@ 40%	2,240
	12,000		
CGT payment			3,520

Working

Basic rate band remaining £(32,400 – 26,000) = £6,400

3

	Six years taper (80%)	*Four years taper (90%)*
	£	£
Gains	16,000	5,000
Less: loss (best use)		(2,500)
Gains before taper relief	16,000	2,500
Taper relief	80%	90%
Gains after taper relief	12,800	2,250

	£
Total gains	15,050
Less: annual exemption	(8,500)
Taxable gains 2005/06	6,550

4

	£
70% × £30,956 (W)	21,669
Less: AE	(8,500)
Taxable gain	13,169

	£		£
CGT to pay:	6,100*	@ 20%	1,220
	7,069	@ 40%	2,828
	13,169		4,048

* (32,400 – 26,300)

Working

	£
Proceeds	40,300
Less: cost	(6,000)
enhancement expenditure	(2,000)
	32,300
Less: indexation allowance:	
£6,000 × 0.167	(1,002)
£2,000 × 0.171	(342)
Indexed gain	30,956

Gain after taper relief (6 April 1998 – 5 April 2005 = 7 years plus additional year = 8 years)

5

	£
Gross proceeds	180,000
Less: selling costs	(2,350)
Net proceeds	177,650
Less: cost	(110,220)
Gain	67,430

Gain after taper relief (3 January 2001 – 2 January 2006 = 5 years) 85% × £67,430 = £57,316

answers to chapter 7: CHARGEABLE GAINS: ADDITIONAL ASPECTS

1

	£
Proceeds	45,000
Cost £8,000 × $\frac{45,000}{45,000+50,000}$	(3,789)
Unindexed gain	41,211
Indexation allowance 0.968 × £3,789	(3,668)
Indexed gain	37,543

Gain after taper relief (6 April 1998 – 5 April 2005 = 7 years plus additional year = 8 years)

	£
70% × £37,543	26,280
Less: AE	(8,500)
Taxable gain	17,780

2 The disposal of an asset between husband and wife gives rise to neither a gain nor a loss, whatever actual price is paid. The effect is that Dora will have the same base cost as Peter, that is £125,000.

3 **Summary**

	Non-business asset (8 years)
	£
Gain (W1)	3,333
Less: loss (W2)	(1,200)
Net gains	2,133

Gain after taper relief

£2,133 × 70% = £1,493

Workings

1) *Ming vase*

	£
Proceeds	8,000
Allowable cost	(2,000)
Unindexed gain	6,000
Indexation allowance 0.872 × 2,000	(1,744)
Indexed gain	4,256

Gain cannot exceed 5/3 × (8,000 – 6,000) = 3,333

Therefore, gain before taper relief = £3,333

Taper relief period is (6 April 1998 – 5 April 2005 = 7 years plus additional year = 8 years)

2) *Leonardo cartoon*

	£
Proceeds (deemed)	6,000
Allowable cost	(7,200)
Allowable loss	(1,200)

Indexation cannot increase a loss, therefore loss = £(1,200)

answers to chapter 8: SHARES

1 Capital gains tax liability

	£
Gain on shares (W1)	13,586
Less: annual exemption	(8,500)
Chargeable gain	5,086

CGT thereon:

£5,086 @ 20% = £1,017

Note.

	£
Income	30,000
Less: personal allowance	(4,895)
Taxable income	25,105

Thus £7,295 of basic rate band remains (£32,400 – £25,105)

Workings

1) *Sale of shares*

a)

	£	£
May 2001 acquisition		
Sale proceeds (1,000 shares) $\frac{1,000}{3,000} \times £27,000$	9,000	
Less: cost	(3,000)	
Gain before taper relief	6,000	
Gain after taper relief (4 years) 90% × 6,000		5,400

B/f		5,400
b) *FA 85 Pool*		
Sale proceeds (2,000 shares)		
$\frac{2,000}{3,000} \times £27,000$	18,000	
Less: cost (W2)	(3,572)	
	14,428	
Less: indexation allowance (W2)	(2,733)	
Indexed gain	11,695	
Gain after taper relief (6 April 1998 – 5 April 2005 = 7 years plus additional year = 8 years) 70% × £11,695		8,186
		13,586

2) *FA 1985 Pool*

	No of shares	*Cost* £	*Indexed cost* £
Purchase	2,000	3,000	3,000
Initial indexation to April 1985 0.158 × 3,000			474
			3,474
Index to November 1985 0.012 × 3,474			42
Purchase	5,000	9,500	9,500
	7,000	12,500	13,016
Index to October 1987 0.073 × 13,016			950
			13,966
Sale	(3,000)	(5,357)	(5,985)
	4,000	7,143	7,981
Index to April 1998 0.580 × 7,981			4,629
			12,610
Sale July 2005 $\frac{2,000}{4,000}$	(2,000)	(3,572)	(6,305)
	2,000	3,571	6,305

The indexation allowance on the July 2005 sale is £(6,305 – 3,572) = £2,733.

2 Gains

10 April 2000 Acquisition

	£
Proceeds $\frac{10,000}{12,000} \times £48,000$	40,000
Less: cost	(29,000)
Gain before taper relief	11,000

Gain after taper relief (10 April 2000 – 9 April 2005 = 5 years) 85% × £11,000 = £9,350

FA 1985 pool

	£
Proceeds $\frac{2,000}{12,000} \times £48,000$	8,000
Less: cost	(2,400)
Unindexed gain	5,600
Less: IA (4,039 – 2,400)	(1,639)
Gain before taper relief	3,961

Gain after taper relief (6 April 1998 – 5 April 2005 = 7 years plus additional year = 8 years)

70% × 3,961 = £2,773

Total gains £(9,350 + 2,773) = £12,123

10 April 2000 Acquisition

	No of shares	*Cost* £
10 April 2000	8,000	29,000
20 September 2000	2,000	–
	10,000	29,000
15 March 2006	(10,000)	(29,000)
C/f	NIL	NIL

FA 1985 pool

	No of shares	*Cost* £	*Indexed cost* £
10 February 1986	12,000	18,000	18,000
Index to April 1998			
0.683 × £18,000			12,294
			30,294
20 September 2000 Bonus	3,000	NIL	NIL
	15,000	18,000	30,294
15 March 2006 Sale	(2,000)	(2,400)	(4,039)
C/f	13,000	15,600	26,255

3

	£	Gains/ (losses) £
Next 30 days		
Proceeds $\frac{2,000}{18,000}$ × £108,000	12,000	
Cost	(11,500)	
		500
No taper relief		
1985 Pool		
Proceeds $\frac{16,000}{18,000}$ × £108,000	96,000	
Cost (W)	(24,400)	
Indexation (W) (27,181 – 24,400)	(2,781)	
	68,819	
Gain after taper relief (6 April 1998 – 5 April 2005 = 7 years plus additional year = 8 years) 70% × £68,819		48,173
Total gains		48,673

Working

1985 Pool

	No of shares	*Cost* £	*Indexed cost* £
9 December 1986: purchase	12,000	4,400	4,400
Index to April 1998: 0.632 × £4,400			2,781
	12,000	4,400	7,181
October 1999 rights (1:3)	4,000	20,000	20,000
	16,000	24,400	27,181
Disposal	(16,000)	(24,400)	(27,181)

answers to chapter 9: PRIVATE RESIDENCES

1 Computation of chargeable gain on sale of house

Period	*Narrative*	*Occupation or deemed occupation (months)*	*Non-occupation (months)*
1 March 1982 to 1 December 1995	Actual occupation	164	
2 December 1995 to 3 July 2002	Absence		79
4 July 2002 to 3 July 2005	Last three years deemed occupation	36	
		200	79
plus:			200
Total ownership period			279

	£
Proceeds (3 July 2005)	270,000
Less: cost	(70,000)
Unindexed gain	200,000
Less: indexation allowance:	
Gain £70,000 × 1.047	(73,290)
	126,710
Less: exemption for main residence 200/279	(90,832)
Chargeable gain	35,878

Tutorial note. The last 36 months of ownership always count as a period of occupation. None of the 79 month period of absence counts as a period of deemed occupation since it was not followed by a period of actual occupation.

answers to chapter 10: ADMINISTRATION AND PAYMENT OF INCOME TAX AND CGT

1 'Tax Help For You'
16 The Road
London
England

John Hunt
22 The Street
Anywhere
England

28 September 2006

Dear John

Income tax return

Further to your letter of 16 September 2006, I am writing to let you know that I will need the following information and documents in order to complete your income tax return.

1) *Forms P60 and P11D*

   Both of these forms should have been supplied to you by your employer. Form P60 will give me details of your salary and tax deducted from it. Form P11D will give me the details I need regarding your company car and private medical insurance.

2) *Bank and Building Society Certificates of annual interest earned*

   These will provide the details I need regarding your taxable interest and the tax deducted from it.

3) Annual pension statement

   This will give me the details I need of your pension payments and of any tax withheld at source from the payments.

4) Receipted subscription notice

   This will show me details of the subscription you have paid.

I do not need any details of either your mortgage payments or of the interest arising on your ISA account. This is because there is no tax relief for mortgage payments and the interest arising on your ISA account is tax free.

Your completed tax return must be submitted to the Revenue by 31 January 2007. Had you wanted the Revenue to calculate your tax for you, you would need to submit your return by 30 September 2006.

Any outstanding tax is due for payment on 31 January 2007. Tax is only normally collected via a PAYE code if the outstanding amount is less than £2,000 and the return has been submitted by 30 September following the tax year concerned.

A fixed penalty of £100 applies if your tax return is not submitted by 31 January 2007. This penalty rises to £200 if the return is more than six months late. Interest is charged on a daily basis in respect of any tax paid late and there is an additional 5% surcharge if tax is paid more than 28 days late.

Finally, in response to the final point in your letter, a husband and wife are taxed independently so there will be no need for us to consider your wife's income when completing your tax return.

I look forward to meeting you but in the meantime, if you have any further queries please do not hesitate to contact me.

Yours sincerely

Peter Jones

PRACTICE EXAM 1 (SPECIMEN PAPER)

UNIT 19

ANSWERS

ANSWERS

SECTION 1

Task 1.1

	£
Car (£28,600 × 22% (W))	6,292
Fuel (£14,400 × 22% (W))	3,168
Loan £20,000 × (5% – 2.5%) (Note)	500
	9,960

Working

Taxable percentage for car and fuel benefit

Emission rating rounded down to the nearest 5 below = 175g/km.
Amount over baseline figure 175 – 140 = 35g/km
Divided by 5 = 7
Taxable percentage = 15% + 7% = 22%

Tutorial note. Take care when you read the dates; the loan was available for the whole of the tax year.

Task 1.2

	Non-savings	*Savings*	*Dividend*	*Total*
	£	£	£	£
Salary	18,500			
Less: pension @ 5%	(925)			
	17,575			
Less: annual subscription	(250)			
	17,325			
Benefits (task 1.1)	9,960			
BSI (gross)		5,200		
Dividends (gross)	–	–	6,000	
	27,285	5,200	6,000	38,485
Less PA	(4,895)			
Total	22,390	5,200	6,000	33,590

Tutorial note. Contributions to an employer's pension scheme are deducted in arriving at taxable income. In contrast, contributions to a personal pension plan are not deducted in computing taxable income. The figure on the P60 issued to Phil Bright will be £(18,500 – 925) = £17,575.

Task 1.3

		£
Tax on non-savings income		
£2,090 × 10%		209.00
£20,300 × 22%		4,466.00
£22,390		
Tax on savings income		
£5,200 × 20%		1,040.00
Tax on dividend income		
£4,810 × 10%		481.00
£1,190 × 32.5%		386.75
£6,000		6,582.75
Less: tax deducted at source	£	
dividends	600	
BSI	1,040	
		(1,640.00)
Net tax liability		4,942.75

Task 1.4

Protecting client confidentiality is crucial. Under no circumstances should the details of a person's tax situation be discussed with another person. You should politely, but firmly, explain to Beryl that you cannot comply with her request, although you would be happy to assist her individually.

Task 1.5

Income for the year ended 5 April 2006

EMPLOYMENT

Fill in these boxes first

Name

Tax reference

If you want help, look up the box numbers in the Notes.

Details of employer

Employer's PAYE reference - may be shown under 'Revenue and Customs office number and reference' on your P60 or 'PAYE reference' on your P45

1.1

Employer's name

1.2

Date employment started
(only if between 6 April 2005 and 5 April 2006)

1.3 / /

Date employment finished
(only if between 6 April 2005 and 5 April 2006)

1.4 / /

Employer's address

1.5

Postcode

Tick box 1.6 if you were a director of the company

1.6

and, if so, tick box 1.7 if it was a close company

1.7

Income from employment

■ ***Money*** *- see Notes, page EN3.*

		Before tax
• Payments from P60 (or P45)	1.8	£ 17,575
• Payments not on P60, etc. - tips	1.9	£
- other payments (excluding expenses entered below and lump sums and compensation payments or benefits entered overleaf)	1.10	£

		Tax taken off
• UK tax taken off payments in boxes 1.8 to 1.10	1.11	£

■ ***Benefits and expenses*** *- see Notes, pages EN3 to EN6. If any benefits connected with termination of employment were received, or enjoyed, after that termination and were from a **former** employer you need to complete Help Sheet IR204, available from the Orderline. Do not enter such benefits here.*

		Amount			Amount
• Assets transferred/ payments made for you	1.12	£	• Vans	1.18	£
• Vouchers, credit cards and tokens	1.13	£	• Interest-free and low-interest loans *see Note for box 1.19, page EN5.*	1.19	£ 500
• Living accommodation	1.14	£	*box 1.20 is not used.*		
• Excess mileage allowance and passenger payments	1.15	£	• Private medical or dental insurance	1.21	£
• Company cars	1.16	£ 6,292	• Other benefits	1.22	£
• Fuel for company cars	1.17	£ 3,168	• Expenses payments received and balancing charges	1.23	£

SA101

Income from employment continued

■ ***Lump sums and compensation payments or benefits including such payments and benefits from a former employer***
Note that 'lump sums' here includes any contributions which your employer made to an unapproved retirement benefits scheme.

*You must read page EN6 of the Notes **before** filling in boxes 1.24 to 1.30.*

Reliefs

• £30,000 exception	1.24	£
• Foreign service and disability	1.25	£
• Retirement and death lump sums	1.26	£

Taxable lump sums

• From box B of *Help Sheet IR204*	1.27	£
• From box K of *Help Sheet IR204*	1.28	£
• From box L of *Help Sheet IR204*	1.29	£
• Tax taken off payments in boxes 1.27 to 1.29 *- leave blank if this tax is included in the box 1.11 figure and tick box 1.30A.*	1.30	Tax taken off £
• Tick this box if you have left box 1.30 blank because the tax is included in the box 1.11 figure	1.30A	

■ ***Foreign earnings not taxable in the UK in the year ended 5 April 2006*** *- see Notes, pages EN6 to EN7* — 1.31 £

■ ***Expenses you incurred in doing your job*** *- see Notes, pages EN7 to EN8.*

• Travel and subsistence costs	1.32	£
• Fixed deductions for expenses	1.33	£
• Professional fees and subscriptions	1.34	£ 250
• Other expenses and capital allowances	1.35	£
• Tick box 1.36 if the figure in box 1.32 includes travel between your home and a permanent workplace	1.36	

■ ***Seafarers' Earnings Deduction*** *(enter the amount of the earnings that attract the deduction, not the tax)* — 1.37 £

■ ***Foreign tax for which tax credit relief not claimed*** — 1.38 £

Student Loans

■ ***Student Loans repaid by deduction by employer*** *- see Notes, page EN8* — 1.39 £

• Tick box 1.39A if your income is under Repayment of Teachers' Loans Scheme — 1.39A

1.40 ***Additional information***

Now fill in any other supplementary Pages that apply to you.
Otherwise, go back to page 2 in your Tax Return and finish filling it in.

SECTION 2

Task 2.1

	No of shares	*Cost* £	*Indexed cost* £
April 1986 – purchase	300	3,000	3,000
IA to May 1990 (£3,000 × 0.224)			672
			3,672
Purchase	500	8,500	8,500
	800	11,500	12,172
June 1992 – bonus issue	160		
	960		
IA to April 1995 (£12,172 × 0.181)			2,203
			14,375
Purchase	1,000	16,000	16,000
	1,960	27,500	30,375
IA to April 1998 (£30,375 × 0.091)			2,764
			33,139
March 2002 – disposal	(400)	(5,612)	(6,763)
	1,560	21,888	26,376
January 2006 – disposal	(1,560)	(21,888)	(26,376)

	£
Proceeds	45,000
Cost	(21,888)
	23,112
IA (26,376 – 21,888)	(4,488)
Chargeable gain before taper relief	18,624

For taper relief purposes the shares have been owned for 8 years. The gain after taper relief is £13,037 (£18,624 × 70%)

Task 2.2

There is no taxable gain or allowable loss as a car is exempt from CGT.

Task 2.3

	£
Proceeds	71,000
Less: cost £80,000 × $\frac{71,000}{71,000+95,000}$	(34,217)
	36,783
IA (£34,217 × 0.062)	(2,121)
Chargeable gain before Taper relief	34,662

For taper relief purposes the land has been owned for eight years (including the additional year) so 70% of the gain is chargeable after taper relief – £24,263

Task 2.4

	£
Rent receivable (£4,800 – £500)	4,300
Loss b/fwd	(1,600)
Net property income	2,700

Task 2.5

	£
Income	
Property income (task 2.4)	2,700
Less: PA (restricted)	(2,700)
Taxable income	–

	Total £
Gains	
Gain on shares (task 2.1)	13,037
Gain on car (task 2.2)	0
Gain on land (task 2.3)	24,263
	37,300
Annual exemption	(8,500)
	28,800

Capital gains tax payable:

	£
£2,090 × 10%	209
£26,710 × 20%	5,342
	5,551

Task 2.6

MEMO

To: Jeanette Alsop
From: Accounting Technician
Date: 1 June 2006
Ref: Late declaration of income

It is always important, when you are dealing with the Revenue, to be as honest as possible. I would therefore recommend that you make a late declaration of income, so that the Revenue has the full picture of your income for 2004/05.

The Revenue will view your mis-declaration as being a submission of an incorrect tax return. Normally, the penalty for this is a charge of up to 100% of the amount of tax underpaid as a result of the incorrect return.

Once the building society interest is taken into account, you will be a 40% taxpayer so you will have made an underpayment of tax. You will therefore need to pay both the underpayment and the penalty.

PRACTICE EXAM 2
(DECEMBER 2003 PAPER)

UNIT 19

ANSWERS

ANSWERS

SECTION 1

Task 1.1

	£
Car benefit (W1)	4,188
Fuel benefit (£14,400 × 24%)	3,456
Loan (£15,000 × (5% – 2%))	450
Entertainment	–
Taxable benefit	8,094

Tutorial notes

1 The company loan was available throughout 2005/06 so there is no need to time apportion it.

2 It is assumed that the reimbursement of the entertainment was a reimbursement of business expenditure.

Working

Car benefit

Excess of emission rating over baseline (170 (round down) - 140) = 30g/km

Divide by 5 = 6

Taxable % = 15% + 6% + 3%(diesel engine) = 24%

	£
24% × £21,200	5,088
Less: contribution (£75 × 12)	(900)
	4,188

Task 1.2

	Non-savings income £	*Savings (excl. Dividend) income* £	*Dividend* £	*Total* £
Salary	40,000			
Taxable benefits	8,094			
Dividends (× 100/90)			1,720	
Interest		–		
	48,094		1,720	49,814
Less: personal allowance	(4,895)	–		
Taxable income	43,199	–	1,720	44,919

Note. Interest arising on an ISA account is tax free.

Task 1.3

	£
Tax on non-savings income	
£2,090 × 10%	209.00
£30,310 × 22%	6,668.20
£10,799 × 40%	4,319.60
	11,196.80
Tax in dividend income	
£1,720 × 32.5%	559.00
	11,755.80
Less: tax credit on dividend (£1,720 × 10%)	(172.00)
	11,583.80

Task 1.4

Provided Joanne is willing to compute her own tax, her tax return for 2005/06 must be submitted by the

a) 31 January 2007
b) 3 months after a notice requiring the return was issued.

If Joanne wishes the Revenue to calculate her tax, her tax return must be submitted by 30 September 2006.

If Joanne submits her return during December 2006 she will have to calculate her own tax but there will be no penalties for late filing.

If Joanne submits her return during February 2007, she will have to calculate her own tax and she will be subject to a £100 penalty for the late filing of the return (assuming a notice requiring the return was issued by 31 October 2006).

Task 1.5

- Net rental income from the letting of property is assessed in a tax year on an accruals basis. This means the rental income due in a tax year is assessed in that year.
- Expenditure is deducted in computing net rental income in the year in which it is payable. In general, revenue expenditure is deductible if it is incurred wholly and exclusively for the letting business.
- Capital expenditure is not deductible. This means the cost of the furniture is not deductible. You may instead claim a wear and tear allowance in respect of the furniture. This is calculated as 10% (rent – water rates – council tax).
- Property income losses can be relieved against other Property income in the same year. Alternatively losses can be carried forward to set against future property income. They cannot be set against other types of income.

Tutorial note. The examiner has said that is it acceptable to answer a question like this using a bullet point list, as above. You will not lose any marks.

Task 1.6

Income for the year ended 5 April 2006

EMPLOYMENT

Fill in these boxes first

Name	Tax reference
Joanne Harper	

If you want help, look up the box numbers in the Notes.

Details of employer

Employer's PAYE reference - may be shown under 'Revenue and Customs office number and reference' on your P60 or 'PAYE reference' on your P45

1.1

Employer's name

1.2 Sunny Dials

Date employment started (only if between 6 April 2005 and 5 April 2006)

1.3 / /

Date employment finished (only if between 6 April 2005 and 5 April 2006)

1.4 / /

Employer's address

1.5

Postcode

Tick box 1.6 if you were a director of the company

1.6 ✓

and, if so, tick box 1.7 if it was a close company

1.7

Income from employment

■ ***Money*** *- see Notes, page EN3.*

		Before tax
• Payments from P60 (or P45)	1.8	£ 40,000
• Payments not on P60, etc. - tips	1.9	£
- other payments (excluding expenses entered below and lump sums and compensation payments or benefits entered overleaf)	1.10	£

		Tax taken off
• UK tax taken off payments in boxes 1.8 to 1.10	1.11	£

■ ***Benefits and expenses*** *- see Notes, pages EN3 to EN6. If any benefits connected with termination of employment were received, or enjoyed, after that termination and were from a* ***former*** *employer you need to complete Help Sheet IR204, available from the Orderline. Do not enter such benefits here.*

		Amount			Amount
• Assets transferred/ payments made for you	1.12	£	• Vans	1.18	£
• Vouchers, credit cards and tokens	1.13	£	• Interest-free and low-interest loans *see Note for box 1.19, page EN5.*	1.19	£ 450
• Living accommodation	1.14	£	*box 1.20 is not used.*		
• Excess mileage allowance and passenger payments	1.15	£	• Private medical or dental insurance	1.21	£
• Company cars	1.16	£ 4,188	• Other benefits	1.22	£
• Fuel for company cars	1.17	£ 3,456	• Expenses payments received and balancing charges	1.23	£ 250

SA101

BS 12/04net TAX RETURN ■ EMPLOYMENT: PAGE E1 *Please turn over*

Income from employment continued

■ ***Lump sums and compensation payments or benefits including such payments and benefits from a former employer***
Note that 'lump sums' here includes any contributions which your employer made to an unapproved retirement benefits scheme.

*You must read page EN6 of the Notes **before** filling in boxes 1.24 to 1.30.*

Reliefs

- £30,000 exception — 1.24 £
- Foreign service and disability — 1.25 £
- Retirement and death lump sums — 1.26 £

Taxable lump sums

- From box B of *Help Sheet IR204* — 1.27 £
- From box K of *Help Sheet IR204* — 1.28 £
- From box L of *Help Sheet IR204* — 1.29 £
- Tax taken off payments in boxes 1.27 to 1.29 *- leave blank if this tax is included in the box 1.11 figure and tick box 1.30A.* — Tax taken off 1.30 £
- Tick this box if you have left box 1.30 blank because the tax is included in the box 1.11 figure — 1.30A

■ ***Foreign earnings not taxable in the UK in the year ended 5 April 2006*** *- see Notes, pages EN6 to EN7* — 1.31 £

■ ***Expenses you incurred in doing your job*** *- see Notes, pages EN7 to EN8.*

- Travel and subsistence costs — 1.32 £
- Fixed deductions for expenses — 1.33 £
- Professional fees and subscriptions — 1.34 £
- Other expenses and capital allowances — 1.35 £ 250
- Tick box 1.36 if the figure in box 1.32 includes travel between your home and a permanent workplace — 1.36

■ ***Seafarers' Earnings Deduction***
(enter the amount of the earnings that attract the deduction, not the tax) — 1.37 £

■ ***Foreign tax for which tax credit relief not claimed*** — 1.38 £

Student Loans

■ ***Student Loans repaid by deduction by employer*** *- see Notes, page EN8* — 1.39 £

- Tick box 1.39A if your income is under Repayment of Teachers' Loans Scheme — 1.39A

1.40 ***Additional information***

Now fill in any other supplementary Pages that apply to you.
Otherwise, go back to page 2 in your Tax Return and finish filling it in.

SECTION 2

Task 2.1

June 2003 acquisition

	£
Disposal $\left(\frac{500}{2,000} \times £61,560\right)$	15,390
Less: cost	(9,800)
Gain	5,590

No taper relief due as these shares have been held for less than three years.

FA 1985 pool

	No of shares	*Cost*	*Indexed cost*
	£	£	£
July 1989	1,000	15,500	15,500
Indexation to August 1993			
£15,500 × 0.223			3,457
			18,957
Purchase	1,500	21,800	21,800
	2,500	37,300	40,757
Indexation to April 1995			
£40,757 × 0.054			2,201
			42,958
Rights issue	500	5,000	5,000
	3,000	42,300	47,958
Indexation to April 1998			
£47,958 × 0.091			4,364
	3,000	42,300	52,322
Less: May 2001 disposal	(800)	(11,280)	(13,952)
Less: March 2006 disposal	(1,500)	(21,150)	(26,161)
Balance c/f	700	9,870	12,209

	£
Disposal $\left(\frac{1,500}{2,000} \times £61,560\right)$	46,170
Less: cost	(21,150)
	25,020
Less: Indexation (£26,161 – £21,150)	(5,011)
Gain	20,009

The shares are a non-business asset that have been held for eight years including the bonus year. 70% of this is chargeable after taper relief.

Task 2.2

The gain arising on disposal of the antique table is **EXEMPT**.

Note. The table is a chattel sold for GROSS PROCEEDS of £6,000 or less.

Task 2.3

	£
Proceeds	101,000
Less: cost £50,000 × $\frac{101,000}{101,000+25,000}$	(40,079)
	60,921
Less: indexation £40,079 × 0.361	(14,469)
Gain before taper relief	46,452

70% of this gain is chargeable after taper relief.

Task 2.4

	70% Gain chargeable	*100% Gain chargeable*
	£	£
Gain on land	46,452	
FA 1985 pool shares	20,009	
June 2001 acquisition		5,590
	66,461	5,590
Less : loss b/f	(14,410)	(5,590)
Net gains	52,051	–

Gains chargeable after taper relief

	£
£52,051 × 70%	36,436
Less: annual exemption	(8,500)
Taxable gain	27,936

Tutorial note. The loss is initially allocated to the gain that attracts the least amount of taper relief, (ie where 100% of the gain is chargeable).

Task 2.5

	Savings (excl. divided) income	Dividend income	Total
	£	£	£
Dividend (× 100/90)		8,500	
Bank interest (× 100/80)	900		
	900	8,500	9,400
Less: personal allowance	(900)	(3,995)	
Taxable income	–	4,505	4,505

Income tax liability

Dividend income

£4,505 × 10% = £450

Basic rate band remaining

(£32,400 – £4,505 = £27,895)

	£
Capital gains tax liability	
£27,895 × 20%	5,579.00
£41 × 40%	16.40
£27,936	5,595.40

Task 2.6

Thank you for your query. You need not be concerned that your tax affairs will not remain private. The firm of Accountants that you use are bound by the ethical guidelines of confidentiality. This means that they may not disclose any details of your affairs to a third party without your consent.

PRACTICE EXAM 3 (JUNE 2004 PAPER)

UNIT 19

ANSWERS

ANSWERS

SECTION 1

Task 1.1

	£
Rental income (£5,000 × 9/12)	3,750
Less: insurance	(450)
10% wear and tear allowance (£3,750 × 10%)	(375)
Net rental income	2,925

Task 1.2

	£	£
Salary		27,000
Accommodation – annual value	5,500	
– additional charge 5% (90,000 – 75,000)	750	
		6,250
Camera (20% × £500 × 6/12)		50
Employment income		33,300

Tutorial notes

1. As the camera was only available for six months of the year, then benefit must be time apportioned.
2. As the accommodation cost over £75,000 an additional charge arises on the excess cost over £75,000.

Task 1.3

	Non-savings income	*Savings (excluding dividend) income*	*Dividend income*	*Total*
	£	£	£	£
Rental income	2,925			
Employment income	33,300			
Dividends (× 100/90)			800	
Building society interest (× 100/80)		460		
	36,225	460	800	37,485
Less: personal allowance	(4,895)			
	31,330	460	800	32,590

Task 1.4

	£
Tax on non-savings income	
£2,090 × 10%	209.00
£29,240 × 22%	6,432.80
Tax on savings (excluding dividend) income	
£460 × 20%	92.00
Tax on dividend income	
£610 × 10%	61.00
£190 × 32.5%	61.75
	6,856.55
Less: tax credit on dividends	(80.00)
PAYE	(4,250.00)
tax on building society interest (20% × £460)	(92.00)
Tax payable	2,434.55

Task 1.5

- To calculate a taxable car benefit the list price of the car is multiplied by a taxable percentage.
- Any capital contribution of up to £5,000 made towards the cost of the car is deducted from the list price for the purpose of computing the benefit.
- The taxable percentage is 15% for cars with CO_2 emissions of 140g/km or less.
- The taxable percentage increases by 1% for every 5g/km that CO_2 emissions exceed the baseline figure of 140 g/km. The maximum percentage is 35%.
- Contributions by Averil for the private use of the car decrease the amount of the taxable benefit.
- The fuel benefit is calculated as £14,400 × the taxable percentage that was used to calculate the car benefit.
- There is no fuel benefit, if no petrol is provided for private use.
- If petrol is provided for private use, the fuel benefit applys in full. There are no deductions for partial contributions towards the cost of private fuel.

Task 1.6

- Three payments must be made in respect of the tax due.
- The first two payments, called payments on account, are paid on 31 July in the tax year and on 31 January following the tax year. They are each equal to 50% of the tax payable in the previous year.

- This means that the 2004/05 payments on account would have been calculated as 50% of the income tax payable for 2003/04.
- The third payment of tax is due on 31 January following the tax year. This is calculated as the difference between the tax payable for the year and the payments on account already made. For 2004/05 it is £780 £(7,580 – 3,400 – 3,400)
- The payments on account for 2005/06 are 50% × income tax payable for 2004/05, ie 50% × £7,580 = £3,790.
- The final payment for 2005/06 will be due on 31 January 2007. It will be the difference between the total amount payable for 2005/06 and the two payments on account of £3,790 each.

SECTION 2

Task 2.1

	£
Sale proceeds	187,500
Less: cost	(65,000)
	122,500
Less: indexation (£65,000 × 0.701)	(45,565)
	76,935
Less: principal private residence (174/242 × £76,935)	(55,317)
Taxable gain	21,618

Gain after taper relief (70% × £21,618) = £15,133

	Actual or (deemed) occupation Months	*Non-occupation* Months
1 October 1985 to 31 January 1988 (actual)	28	
1 February 1988 to 31 January 1990 (work abroad)	24	
1 February 1990 to 31 March 1994 (actual)	50	
1 April 1994 to 30 November 2002 (any reason)	36	68
1 December 2002 to 30 November 2005 (last 36 months)	36	
	174	68

Task 2.2

January 2001

	No of shares	*Cost* £
January 2001	6,000	140,160
Rights issue	600	4,800
	6,600	144,960

	£
Disposal proceeds	75,800
Less: cost $\left(£144,960 \times \frac{2,500}{6,600}\right)$	(54,909)
Gain before taper relief	20,891

Gain after taper relief (4 years – 90%)

£20,891 × 90% = £18,802

Task 2.3

	£
Proceeds	15,000
Less: cost	(7,000)
enhancement expenditure	(1,000)
	7,000
Less: indexation (£7,000 × 0.824)	(5,768)
	1,232

Gain after taper relief (70% × £1,232) = £862

Task 2.4

	£
House (task 2.1)	15,133
Shares (task 2.2)	18,802
Table (task 2.3)	862
	34,797
Less: Annual exemption	(8,500)
Taxable gain	26,297

Taxable income

	£
Company pension	24,000
Less: personal allowance	(4,895)
Taxable income	19,105

Interest arising on the ISA is exempt from tax.

£13,295 (£32,400 – £19,105)of the basic rate band remains.

		£
CGT	£13,295 × 20%	2,659.00
	£13,002 × 40%	5,200.80
	£26,297	7,859.80

Task 2.5

- Losses from 2004/05 can be set against gains before taper relief in 2005/06.
- The losses, are set against gains with the lowest amount of taper relief (ie where the highest percentage of the gain remains chargeable). Taper relief is then applied.
- In this case the loss should be set against the gain on the shares:

	£	£
Table		
Gain after taper relief		862
House		
Gain after taper relief		15,133
Shares		
Gain before taper relief	20,891	
Less: losses b/f	(6,000)	
	14,891	
Gain after taper relief (£14,891 × 90%)		13,402
		29,397
Less: annual exemption		(8,500)
Taxable gain		20,897

		£
CGT	£13,295 × 20%	2,659.00
	£7,602 × 40%	3,040.80
	20,897	5,699.80

Tutorial note. The examiner has indicated that it is acceptable to answer a written question in bullet point form, as here.

PRACTICE EXAM 4 (DECEMBER 2004 PAPER)

UNIT 19

ANSWERS

ANSWERS

SECTION 1

Task 1.1

a)

	£
Car benefit (18% × £18,000)	3,240
Less: contribution for private use (£100 × 12)	(1,200)
	2,040
Fuel benefit (£14,400 × 18%)	2,592
	4,632
Computer (20% × £1,200 × 4/12)(2)	–
	4,632

Tutorial notes

1) The first £500 of taxable benefit arising in respect of the private use of a computer is tax exempt. It was important to clearly state this on the exam paper in order to gain credit for knowing this. If you merely ignored the computer you would not get the mark.

2) The contribution for the private use of the car can be deducted in computing the car benefit.

Working

Car benefit: 157g/km rounded down = 155g/km.

Amount above baseline: 157g/km – 140g/km = 15g/km.

Divide by 5: 15/5 = 3

Taxable percentage = 15% + 3% = 18%

b)

	£
Employment income	28,000
Less: pension contribution (6% × £28,000)	(1,680)
Annual subscriptions	(160)
Taxable benefits (a)	4,632
Net employment income	30,792

Task 1.2

	Non-savings income £	*Dividend income* £	*Total* £
Net employment income	30,792		
Dividends (× 100/90)		850	
	30,792	850	31,642
Less: personal allowance	(4,895)		
	25,897	850	26,747

Tutorial note. Interest arising on an ISA is exempt from tax.

Task 1.3

	£
Tax on non-savings income	
£2,090 × 10%	209.00
£23,807 × 22%	5,237.54
£25,897	5,446.54
Tax on dividend income	
£850 × 10%	85.00
	5,531.54

Task 1.4

Joshua should be assured that the ethical guideline of confidentiality applies to Chartered Accountants and this guideline means that his personal information will remain confidential within the firm.

Task 1.5

- Employer provided accommodation may constitute a taxable benefit. The basic benefit is equal to the annual value of the property.
- There is an additional benefit – the accommodation cost in excess of £75,000 equal to (cost – £75,000) × 5%.
- However if the accommodation is job related, no taxable benefit arises. Broadly, accommodation is job related if you are required to live in it in order to fulfil your job.
- If the accommodation is not job related you will be taxed on all running costs paid by your employer. If, however the accommodation is job related, the amount taxed in respect of running costs is restricted to an amount equal to 10% of your net earnings. Your net earnings are your salary less your pension contribution.

Tutorial notes.

1 The examiner has said that you can answer a question like this in bullet point form as shown above.

2 Ensure you answer the question asked in a written question like this.

SECTION 2

Task 2.1

FA 1985 pool shares

		No of shares	Cost	Indexed cost
			£	£
September 1984		1,000	2,000	2,000
Index to April 1985	£2,000 × 0.052			104
Pool starts		1,000	2,000	2,104
Index to December 1990	£2,104 × 0.371			781
		1,000	2,000	2,885
Addition		1,000	3,000	3,000
		2,000	5,000	5,885
Index to July 1995	0.148 × £5,885			871
				6,756
Addition		1,000	4,500	4,500
		3,000	9,500	11,256
Index to April 1998	0.091 × £11,256			1,024
Pool closes		3,000	9,500	12,280

	£
Disposal proceeds	15,000
Less: cost	(9,500)
Less: indexation (£12,280 – £9,500)	(2,780)
Chargeable gain before taper relief	2,720

Tutorial note. It is very important that you can deal with the construction of the FA 1985 pool, as this is a frequently examined topic.

Task 2.2

Post April 1998 acquisition

	No of shares	Cost
		£
January 2002	3,000	14,800
August 2004 – bonus	600	–
	3,600	14,800

	£
Disposal proceeds	25,500
Less: cost	(14,800)
Chargeable gain before taper relief	10,700

Task 2.3

Post April 1998 acquisition

	No of shares	*Cost*
		£
January 2003	6,000	18,000
December 2003 – Rights issue	120	900
	6,120	18,900

	£
Proceeds	12,000
Less: cost $\left(£18,900 \times \frac{5,000}{6,120}\right)$	(15,441)
Allowable loss	(3,441)

Tutorial note. Rights issue shares must always be pooled with the shares to which they relate.

Task 2.4

The gain arising on the sale of the picture is exempt as the picture is a chattel sold for less than £6,000.

Task 2.5

The loss on the sale of C Ltd shares is set against the gain on the B Ltd shares, as these shares attract the lowest amount of taper relief (ie the highest percentage of this gain is chargeable):

	A Ltd	*B Ltd*
	£	£
Gain before taper relief	2,720	10,700
Less: loss		(3,441)
	2,720	7,259
Gains after taper relief 70%/95%	1,904	6,896

	£
Total gains (£1,904 + £6,896)	8,800
Less: annual exemption	(8,500)
Net taxable gain	300

Tutorial note. The examiner has said that the understanding of how capital losses and taper relief works will be frequently examined in this unit.

Task 2.6

	£
Property income (£500 × 12)	6,000
Agency fees (10%)	(600)
Rates and repairs	(1,250)
	4,150
Less: loss b/f	(860)
Net rental income	3,290

Task 2.7

a)

	£
Property income	3,290
Less: personal Allowance	(3,290)
Taxable income	Nil

Therefore the total income tax liability for the year is £NIL.

b) Net taxable gain (task 2.5) =£300
Tax @ 10% = £30

Task 2.8

Income for the year ended 5 April 2006

LAND AND PROPERTY

Fill in these boxes first

Name: Sarah Cartney

Tax reference:

If you want help, look up the box numbers in the Notes.

Are you claiming Rent a Room relief for gross rents of £4,250 or less?
(Or £2,125 if the claim is shared?)
Read the Notes on page LN2 to find out
- whether you can claim Rent a Room relief; and
- how to claim relief for gross rents over £4,250

Yes ☐ — If 'Yes', tick box. If this is your only income from UK property, you have finished these Pages

Is your income from furnished holiday lettings?
If not applicable, please turn over and fill in Page L2 to give details of your property income

Yes ☐ — If 'Yes', tick box and fill in boxes 5.1 to 5.18 before completing Page L2

Furnished holiday lettings

- **Income from furnished holiday lettings** — 5.1 £

■ ***Expenses*** (furnished holiday lettings only)

- Rent, rates, insurance, ground rents etc. — 5.2 £
- Repairs, maintenance and renewals — 5.3 £
- Finance charges, including interest — 5.4 £
- Legal and professional costs — 5.5 £
- Costs of services provided, including wages — 5.6 £
- Other expenses — 5.7 £ — total of boxes 5.2 to 5.7: 5.8 £

Net profit (put figures in brackets if a loss) — box 5.1 *minus* box 5.8: 5.9 £

■ ***Tax adjustments***

- Private use — 5.10 £
- Balancing charges — 5.11 £ — box 5.10 + box 5.11: 5.12 £
- Capital allowances — 5.13 £
- Tick box 5.13A if box 5.13 includes enhanced capital allowances for environmentally friendly expenditure — 5.13A ☐

Profit for the year (copy to box 5.19). If loss, enter '0' in box 5.14 and put the loss in box 5.15 — boxes 5.9 + 5.12 *minus* box 5.13: 5.14 £

Loss for the year (if you have entered '0' in box 5.14) — boxes 5.9 + 5.12 *minus* box 5.13: 5.15 £

■ ***Losses***

- Loss offset against 2005-06 total income — 5.16 £
- Loss - relief to be calculated by reference to earlier years — see Notes, page LN4: 5.17 £
- Loss offset against other income from property (copy to box 5.38) — see Notes, page LN4: 5.18 £

SA105

BS 12/04net — TAX RETURN ■ LAND AND PROPERTY: PAGE L1 — *Please turn over*

Other property income

Income

	Box	£	Box	£
Furnished holiday lettings profits (copy from box 5.14)	5.19			
Rents and other income from land and property	5.20	6,000	5.21 (Tax taken off)	
Chargeable premiums	5.22			
Reverse premiums	5.22A		5.23 (boxes 5.19 + 5.20 + 5.22 + 5.22A)	6,000

Expenses (do not include figures you have already put in boxes 5.2 to 5.7 on Page L1)

	Box	£	Box	£
Rent, rates, insurance, ground rents etc.	5.24	1,250		
Repairs, maintenance and renewals	5.25			
Finance charges, including interest	5.26			
Legal and professional costs	5.27	600		
Costs of services provided, including wages	5.28			
Other expenses	5.29		5.30 (total of boxes 5.24 to 5.29)	1,850
Net profit (put figures in brackets if a loss)			5.31 (box 5.23 *minus* box 5.30)	4,150

Tax adjustments

	Box	£	Box	£
Private use	5.32			
Balancing charges	5.33		5.34 (box 5.32 + box 5.33)	
Rent a Room exempt amount	5.35			
Capital allowances	5.36			
Tick box 5.36A if box 5.36 includes a claim for 100% capital allowances for flats over shops	5.36A			
Tick box 5.36B if box 5.36 includes enhanced capital allowances for environmentally friendly expenditure	5.36B			
Landlord's energy saving allowance	5.36C			
10% wear and tear	5.37			
Furnished holiday lettings losses (from box 5.18)	5.38		5.39 (total of boxes 5.35 to box 5.38)	
Adjusted profit (if loss enter '0' in box 5.40 and put the loss in box 5.41)			5.40 (boxes 5.31 + 5.34 *minus* box 5.39)	4,150
Adjusted loss (if you have entered '0' in box 5.40)	5.41 (boxes 5.31 + 5.34 *minus* box 5.39)			
Loss brought forward from previous year			5.42	860
Profit for the year			5.43 (box 5.40 *minus* box 5.42)	3,290

Losses etc

	Box	£
Loss offset against total income (read the note on page LN8)	5.44	
Loss to carry forward to following year	5.45	
Tick box 5.46 if these Pages include details of property let jointly	5.46	
Tick box 5.47 if **all** property income ceased in the year to 5 April 2006 **and** you don't expect to receive such income again, in the year to 5 April 2007	5.47	

Now fill in any other supplementary Pages that apply to you. Otherwise, go back to page 2 of your Tax Return and finish filling it in.

BS 12/04net TAX RETURN ■ LAND AND PROPERTY: PAGE L2

PRACTICE EXAM 5

UNIT 19

ANSWERS

ANSWERS

SECTION 1

Task 1.1

	£	£
Rents accrued		26,400
Less: not recoverable		(1,100)
Net rents		25,300
Less: repairs	500	
interest	5,000	
agent's fees	1,500	
wear and tear – 10% × £25,300	2,530	
		(9,530)
		15,770
Less: loss b/f		(1,300)
Taxable rental income		14,470

Task 1.2

	£
Car benefit (W1)	4,200
Fuel benefit (W2)	NIL
Business travel reimbursed (W3)	NIL
Mobile phone (W4)	NIL
Laptop computer (W5)	NIL
Total taxable benefits	4,200

Workings

1 Excess of emission rating over baseline (190 (rounded down) – 140) = 50

Divided by 5 = 10
Add 3% for diesel car
Taxable % = 15 + 10 + 3 = 28%

28% × £15,000 = £4,200

2 No fuel benefit as private fuel cost fully reimbursed.

3 No taxable benefit on reimbursement of business expenses.

4 Provision of mobile phone is an exempt benefit.

5 Cost £1,500 × 20% = £300

Below minimum taxable benefit of £500 so no charge arises.

Task 1.3

	Non-savings income £	*Savings (excl dividend) income* £	*Dividend income* £	*Total* £
Salary	28,000			
Taxable benefits (1.2)	4,200			
	32,200			
Rental income (1.1)	14,470			
Interest £600 × 100/80		750		
Dividends £1,800 × 100/90			2,000	
	46,670	750	2,000	49,420
Less: PA	(4,895)			
Taxable income	41,775	750	2,000	44,525

Task 1.4

Income for the year ended 5 April 2006

LAND AND PROPERTY

Name: Sally Welch

Tax reference:

Fill in these boxes first

If you want help, look up the box numbers in the Notes.

Are you claiming Rent a Room relief for gross rents of £4,250 or less?
(Or £2,125 if the claim is shared?)
Read the Notes on page LN2 to find out
- whether you can claim Rent a Room relief; and
- how to claim relief for gross rents over £4,250

Yes ☐ — If 'Yes', tick box. If this is your only income from UK property, you have finished these Pages

Is your income from furnished holiday lettings?
If not applicable, please turn over and fill in Page L2 to give details of your property income

Yes ☐ — If 'Yes', tick box and fill in boxes 5.1 to 5.18 before completing Page L2

Furnished holiday lettings

• Income from furnished holiday lettings		5.1 £
■ ***Expenses*** (furnished holiday lettings only)		
• Rent, rates, insurance, ground rents etc.	5.2 £	
• Repairs, maintenance and renewals	5.3 £	
• Finance charges, including interest	5.4 £	
• Legal and professional costs	5.5 £	
• Costs of services provided, including wages	5.6 £	
• Other expenses	5.7 £	total of boxes 5.2 to 5.7 — 5.8 £
Net profit (put figures in brackets if a loss)		box 5.1 *minus* box 5.8 — 5.9 £
■ ***Tax adjustments***		
• Private use	5.10 £	
• Balancing charges	5.11 £	box 5.10 + box 5.11 — 5.12 £
• Capital allowances	5.13 £	
• Tick box 5.13A if box 5.13 includes enhanced capital allowances for environmentally friendly expenditure	5.13A ☐	
Profit for the year (copy to box 5.19). If loss, enter '0' in box 5.14 and put the loss in box 5.15		boxes 5.9 + 5.12 *minus* box 5.13 — 5.14 £
Loss for the year (if you have entered '0' in box 5.14)	boxes 5.9 + 5.12 *minus* box 5.13 — 5.15 £	
■ ***Losses***		
• Loss offset against 2005-06 total income	5.16 £	
• Loss - relief to be calculated by reference to earlier years	see Notes, page LN4 — 5.17 £	
• Loss offset against other income from property (copy to box 5.38)	see Notes, page LN4 — 5.18 £	

SA105

BS 12/04net

Please turn over

Other property income

Income

Furnished holiday lettings profits	5.19 (copy from box 5.14)	£				
Rents and other income from land and property	5.20	£ 25,300	5.21 (Tax taken off)	£		
Chargeable premiums	5.22	£				
Reverse premiums	5.22A	£			5.23 (boxes 5.19 + 5.20 + 5.22 + 5.22A)	£ 25,300

Expenses (do not include figures you have already put in boxes 5.2 to 5.7 on Page L1)

Rent, rates, insurance, ground rents etc.	5.24	£		
Repairs, maintenance and renewals	5.25	£ 500		
Finance charges, including interest	5.26	£ 5,000		
Legal and professional costs	5.27	£		
Costs of services provided, including wages	5.28	£		
Other expenses	5.29	£ 1,500	5.30 (total of boxes 5.24 to 5.29)	£ 7,000
Net profit (put figures in brackets if a loss)			5.31 (box 5.23 *minus* box 5.30)	£ 18,300

Tax adjustments

Private use	5.32	£		
Balancing charges	5.33	£	5.34 (box 5.32 + box 5.33)	£
Rent a Room exempt amount	5.35	£		
Capital allowances	5.36	£		
Tick box 5.36A if box 5.36 includes a claim for 100% capital allowances for flats over shops	5.36A			
Tick box 5.36B if box 5.36 includes enhanced capital allowances for environmentally friendly expenditure	5.36B			
Landlord's energy saving allowance	5.36C	£		
10% wear and tear	5.37	£ 2,530		
Furnished holiday lettings losses (from box 5.18)	5.38	£	5.39 (total of boxes 5.35 to box 5.38)	£ 2,530
Adjusted profit (if loss enter '0' in box 5.40 and put the loss in box 5.41)			5.40 (boxes 5.31 + 5.34 *minus* box 5.39)	£ 15,770
Adjusted loss (if you have entered '0' in box 5.40)	5.41 (boxes 5.31 + 5.34 *minus* box 5.39)	£		
Loss brought forward from previous year			5.42	£ 1,300
Profit for the year			5.43 (box 5.40 *minus* box 5.42)	£ 14,470

Losses etc

Loss offset against total income (read the note on page LN8)	5.44	£
Loss to carry forward to following year	5.45	£
Tick box 5.46 if these Pages include details of property let jointly	5.46	
Tick box 5.47 if **all** property income ceased in the year to 5 April 2006 **and** you don't expect to receive such income again, in the year to 5 April 2007	5.47	

Now fill in any other supplementary Pages that apply to you.
Otherwise, go back to page 2 of your Tax Return and finish filling it in.

Task 1.5

	£	£
Non savings income		
£2,090 × 10%		209.00
30,310 × 22%		6,668.20
(£400 × 100/78 × 12) = £6,154 × 22% (personal pension)		1,353.88
£3,221 × 40%		1,288.40
Savings (excl. divis) income		
£750 × 40%		300.00
Dividend income		
£2,000 × 32½%		650.00
		10,469.48
Less: PAYE	4,874	
tax deducted on BI £750 × 20%	150	
tax credit on dividend £2,000 × 10%	200	
		(5,224.00)
Tax payable		5,245.48

Task 1.6

Notes for Sally Welch

Sally has a liability of £5,245.48 for 2005/06 payable by self assessment.

She has already made a payment of $\frac{£4,500}{2}$ = £2,250 on 31 January 2006.

She will make a further payment of £2,250 on 31 July 2006.

The balancing payment of £(5,245.48 – 4,500) = £745.48 will be due on 31 January 2007.

She will also have to make a first payment on account for 2006/07 of:

$\frac{£5,245.48}{2}$ = £2,622.74

on 31 January 2007 and a further payment of the same amount on 31 July 2007.

SECTION 2

Task 2.1

FA 1985 pool

	No of shares	*Cost* £	*Indexed cost* £
March 1994 Acquisition	10,000	5,000	5,000
Indexed rise to April 1998			
0.141 × 5,000			705
			5,705
August 2001 Bonus 1 for 5	2,000		
	12,000		
May 2005 Sale	(6,000)	(2,500)	(2,853)
C/f	6,000	2,500	2,852

Gain on sale

	£
Proceeds	13,800
Less: cost	(2,500)
Unindexed gain	11,300
Less: indexation (2,853 – 2,500)	(353)
Indexed gain	10,947

Owned from April 1998 to May 2005 (7 whole years plus bonus year = 8 years)

Task 2.2

Gain on land

	£
Proceeds	30,000
Less: cost	
$\frac{30,000}{30,000+70,000} \times 50,000$	(15,000)
Gain	15,000

Owned from September 2000 to August 2005 (4 whole years)

Task 2.3

Loss on vase

	£
Proceeds (deemed)	6,000
Less: cost	(7,500)
Loss	(1,500)

Task 2.4

Taxable gains

	Seven years taper £	*Four years taper* £
Shares	10,947	
Land		15,000
Less: loss on vase (best use)		(1,500)
Gains before taper relief	10,947	13,500
Taper relief	70%	90%
Gains after taper relief	7,663	12,150

	£
Total gains	19,813
Less: annual exemption	(8,500)
Taxable gains	11,313

Task 2.5

	£
Capital gains tax payable	
£7,295 (W) × 20%	1,459.00
£4,018 × 40%	1,607.20
CGT due	3,066.20

Working

	£
Earnings	30,000
Less: PA	(4,895)
Taxable income	25,105

Basic rate band remaining

	£
Basic rate band limit	32,400
Less: taxable income	(25,105)
Basic rate band remaining	7,295

Task 2.6

Dear Roger

The gain on the sale of the house can be reduced by a number of reliefs.

The first is called principal private residence relief. It applies because you have lived in the house as your only or main home for part of the time that you have owned it. You can count the 10 years of actually living in the house, plus the last 3 years of ownership. This makes a total of 13 years out of 20 years and this proportion of the gain (£130,000) will be exempt, leaving £70,000 of gain not covered by this relief.

The gain is further reduced to 70% of this gain because of the operation of taper relief. Taper relief is a relief for how long you have owned the asset. After taper relief, £49,000 of the gain will be left in charge.

Finally, you are entitled to an annual exemption of £8,500.

After all these reliefs, the taxable gain will be £40,500.

Yours sincerely

A Trainee

INDEX

ORDER FORM: AAT Companions

To: BPP Professional Education, Aldine House, Aldine Place, London W12 8AW

Mr/Mrs/Ms (name): ______________________

Daytime delivery address: ______________________

______________________ Postcode: __________

Daytime Tel No: __________ Email: __________

		Course	Revision	Combined
Foundation				
Units 1-4		☐ £21.95	☐ £13.95	
Office Skills (Units 21, 22, 23)				☐ £16.95
Intermediate				
Unit 5	Financial Records and Accounts	☐ £14.95	☐ £11.95	
Units 6&7	Cost Information and Reports & Returns	☐ £16.95	☐ £12.95	
Technician				
Units 8&9	Managing Performance and Controlling Resources	☐ £15.95	☐ £12.95	
Unit 10	Managing Accounting Systems and People			☐ £16.95
Unit 11	Drafting Financial Statements (12/05 exam)	☐ £15.95	☐ £12.95	
Unit 11	Drafting Financial Statements (6/06 exam)	☐ £15.95	☐ £12.95	
Unit 15	Cash Management and Control			☐ £16.95
Unit 17	Implementing Auditing Procedures	☐ £15.95	☐ £12.95	
Unit 18	Business Taxation (FA2004)			☐ £16.95
Unit 19	Personal Taxation (FA2004)			☐ £16.95
Unit 18	Business Taxation (FA2005) (8/05)			☐ £16.95
Unit 19	Personal Taxation (FA2005) (8/05)			☐ £16.95
	Sub total:	£	£	£
	Grand total (including Postage & Packing):	£		

Postage & Packing: UK: £3 per item up to the value of £12 per order. Europe: £6 for first item then £4 for each extra item. Rest of world: £20 for first item then £10 for each extra item.

I enclose a cheque for £ __________ **(made payable to *BPP Professional Education*)** OR

Please charge my Mastercard / Visa

Card number ☐☐☐☐☐☐☐☐☐☐☐☐☐☐☐☐

Expiry Date __________ Start Date __________

Issue Number (Switch only) __________